PRAISE FOR *THE END OF STO*

"Stephanie Riggs' *End of Storytelling* is what every creator working across pioneering storytelling formats needs to read. It's a perfect balance between historical context and pragmatic approaches, bringing insight across a convergence of disciplines that help lay the crucial groundwork to approaching these new mediums natively. These approaches and thought processes will help our industry progress in a much needed direction."

Yelena Rachitsky, Executive Producer of Experiences, Oculus

"Provocative, illuminating and exciting. I love the idea of transforming storytelling through the creation of story worlds so the premise was particularly intriguing and one that provided a great deal of thought and introspection. I especially loved the stunning graphics and imagery which took everything to a whole other level."

Michael Jung, Executive Creative Director, Walt Disney Imagineering

Dare you master the Storyplex? This book will show you how. With *The End of Storytelling*, Stephanie Riggs emerges as a 21st century Marshall McLuhan, proving that the medium is so much more than just a message. Read this and understand how technology merges reality and imagination into the magic of experience.

Jesse Schell, Distinguished Professor of Entertainment Technology, Carnegie Mellon University; CEO, Schell Games

"At Refinery29, we have a mission to change the way people see the world, to shake up the status quo, to reflect the world we are seeing around us. Stephanie embodies that vision and has enhanced our ability to do that by creating immersive experiences that reflect so many perspectives and voices and provide greater connection and understanding."

Amy Emmerich, President of North America & Chief Content Officer, Refinery29

"Visually stunning, contextually perfect, Stephanie has written a definitive, must have guide into the future that is now in storytelling. *The End of Storytelling* gives us the how, where, when and why of how to tell immersive stories that are now forever here. Run, don't walk to get a copy of your blueprint, a map on how to tell compelling stories in an age where enabling technological disruptions are permanent."
Adaora Udoji, Director of Corporate Innovation, RLab

"Stephanie's extensive experience across corporations, start-ups, non-profit, and academia creates a unique perspective that has the potential to evolve how immersive creators think about and develop stories in a profound way."
Jake Zim, SVP of Virtual Reality, Sony Pictures Entertainment

"What makes *The End of Storytelling* by Stephanie Riggs so exciting is that it takes the reader on a wonderful journey into the beginning of something new."
Kay Meseberg, Head of Mission Innovation, ARTE

"Riggs possesses a rare interdisciplinary dexterity that allows her to break new ground in conceptualizing and crafting narratives in immersive technology. With *The End of Storytelling*, she presents innovative concepts in a way that makes even the most academic concepts accessible, paving the way for the future students and creators."
Jerome Solomon, Conference Chair, ACM SIGGRAPH 2017

"*The End of Storytelling* is a transformative experience that enlightens Creatives in what traditional narratives have evolved to in the immersive space. This immaculately designed and crafted experience should be on the coffee table of any storyteller of the future. It's very exciting to see where our future is taking us."
Jonathan Jirjis, Director/Producer, One Club

THE END OF STORYTELLING

THE END OF STORYTELLING

THE FUTURE OF NARRATIVE IN THE STORYPLEX

STEPHANIE RIGGS

BEAT MEDIA GROUP

Book design and illustrations by Maya P. Lim

First print edition March 2019

Paperback ISBN 978-1-7329559-2-9
Ebook ISBN 978-1-7329559-1-2

Published by Beat Media Group
www.theendofstorytelling.com

FOR KAREN ANN FUNDERBURK

■ ■ ■ ■ ■ ■   ■ ■ ■ ■ ■   ■ ■ ■ ■

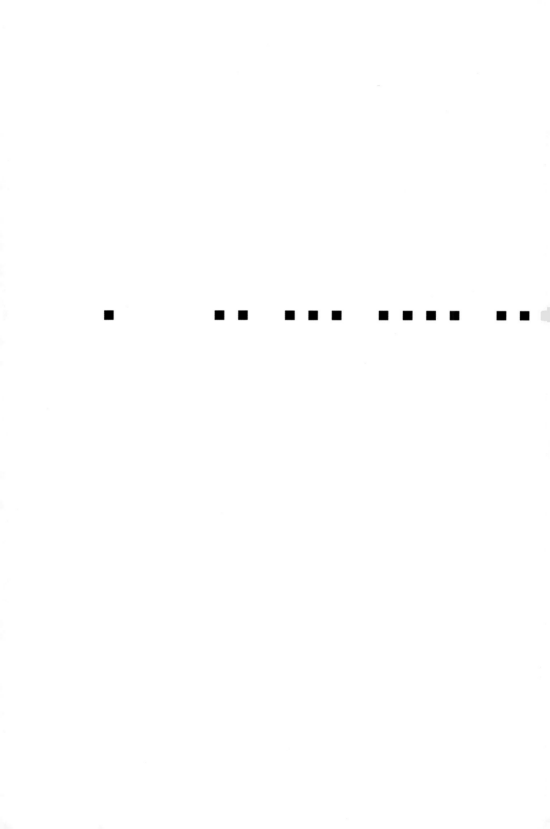

CONTENTS

- -

01 PROLOGUE:
AT THE EDGE OF THE
KNOWN UNIVERSE

39 IMMERSIVE
TECHNOLOGY
CHEATSHEET

57   01: THE STORYTELLING PROBLEM

97   02: WHAT'S OLD IS NEW AGAIN

135   03: THE STORYPLEX

213   ENDNOTES

PROLOGUE

AT THE EDGE OF THE
KNOWN UNIVERSE

THE BOOK.

AN *archaic* MEDIUM FOR EXPLORING IMMERSIVE THINKING. IDEAS TRAPPED IN PAGES, REACHING FOR THE OUTER BOUNDARIES OF THE UNIVERSE.

AND SO THE PAGE TURNS...

1940. QUEENS, NEW YORK.

1940. QUEENS, NEW YORK. A young patent clerk named Chester Carlton approaches 20 major photographic manufacturers with an invention to dramatically improve the process of duplicating documents.

At the time, businesses made copies by sending original documents to an off-site laboratory to undergo an expensive photographic process. This took days.

DUPLICATION PROCESS, 1940

- Compile documents to be copied
- Courier them off-site
- Photo laboratory intakes the documents
- Cameras snap film of each page
- Each photo is chemically developed on specialized paper
- Developed copies held to dry
- Pages are re-collated
- Courier delivers copies back to office

Chester Carlson's invention created a **NEARLY INSTANTANEOUS COPY**, without the need for wet chemicals and expensive specialized paper.

Fig. 1 ←→

23
21 20
22

IBM was one of the few
companies that invited Carlson
to present his idea to their team.
In their offices, Carlson opened his homemade kit of
coated microscope plates and dusting powder.

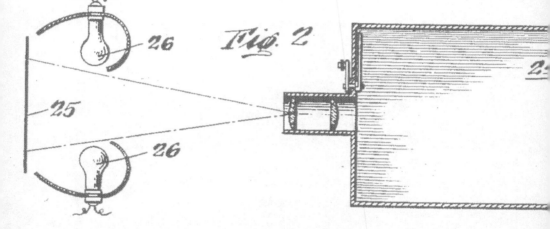

Fig. 2

26
25
26
2:

Instead of taking a photograph, the CalTech graduate
combined principles of physics and chemistry to
transfer an image from a plate to wax paper in
seconds through electrostatic charge. He called it
"electrophotography." It
was a crude image, hardly
the clear picture created by
familiar traditional photography, but it worked.

26 *Fig. 2a*
27 28
20 21
22

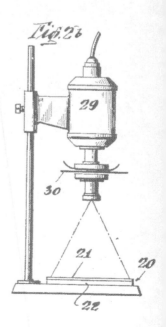

Fig. 2b

29

30

21 20
22

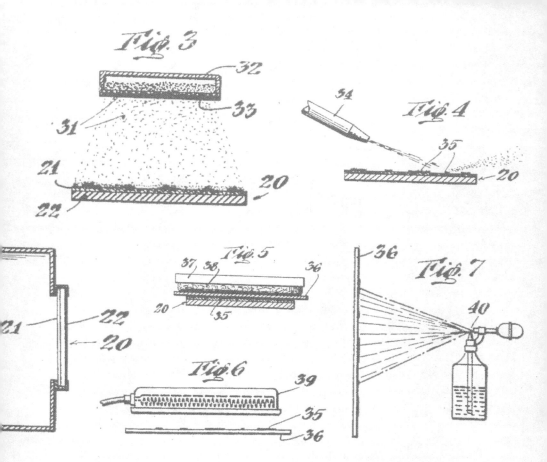

After the demonstration, the executives did not ask a single question. They didn't say anything to Carlson. Instead, they all stood up and left the room.

IBM, General Electric, RCA, Eastman Kodak, and the US Government all turned their backs on the biggest revolution in printing since the Gutenberg press and the chance to be the cornerstone of a multi-billion-dollar industry. It was an obscure paper manufacturer who would spend decades, and risk their entire business, to realize a manufacturable version of Carlson's invention and ultimately become Xerox Corporation, one of the most powerful companies in the world.

WHY DID STATE-OF-THE-ART COMPANIES AND BRILLIANT SCIENTISTS MISS THE REVOLUTION?

They were unprepared for the possibility of a radically different approach.

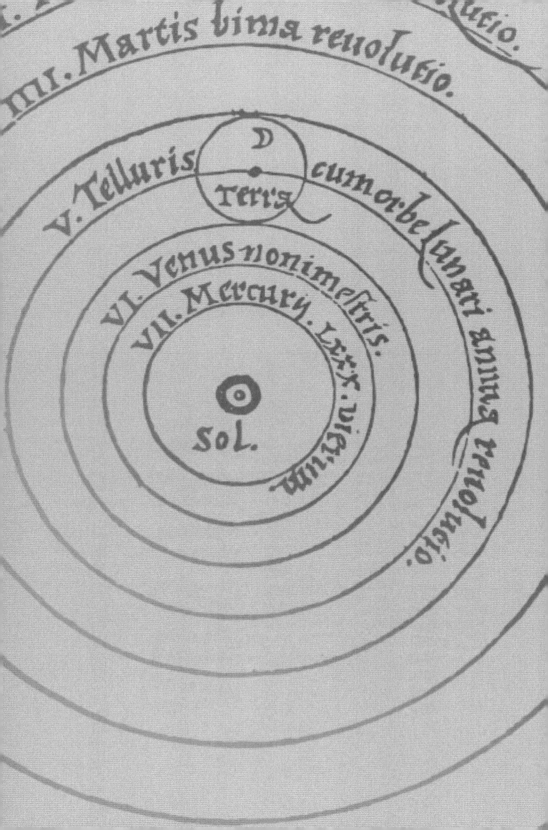

Carlson's electrostatic charge had nothing to do with photography as they knew it.

The concept of using photons and electricity to make copies had "almost no foundation in previous scientific work," according to Xerox physicist Dr. Harold E. Clark. "Chet put together a rather odd lot of phenomena, each of which was obscure in itself and none of which had previously been related in anyone's thinking."

As Carlson recalled from those early demonstrations, "highly trained engineers dismissed it as unworthy of serious consideration without actually understanding the situation."

A WELL-INTEGRATED PARADIGM CAN BECOME SO CONVINCING THAT EVEN THE POSSIBILITY OF ALTERNATIVES SEEMS ABSURD

Established paradigms with a well-refined process and predictable results inhibit even the most brilliant minds from being able to grasp new concepts.

The revered mathematical physicist Lord Kelvin wrote, "I have not the smallest molecule of faith in aerial navigation other than ballooning." Yet today our reality includes jumbo jets, helicopters, and rocket ships that reach outer space.

Charles Darwin wrote in his pivotal work, *On the Origin of Species*, "Although I am fully convinced of the truth of the views given in this volume...I by no means expect to convince experienced naturalists whose minds are stocked with a multitude of facts all viewed, during a long course of years, from a point of view directly opposite mine."

When German physicist Max Planck first introduced the concept of quanta, he initially thought of the variable as nothing more than a "mathematical assumption" created out of desperation to account for inconsistencies observed in classical physics. It was Albert Einstein who would elaborate on Planck's solution to form a cohesive theory of photoelectricity and write the paper that inspired young Chester Carlson's invention.

Planck couldn't grasp the importance of his own discovery for the same reason that photographic manufacturers couldn't see the value in Carlson's

invention: it didn't fit their understanding of how the world worked.

■ ■ ■

In 2017, I consulted on a virtual reality project being developed by a non-profit company in collaboration with GoogleVR. They wanted to build an educational tool against bullying for high-school students. Nobody on the non-profit team had developed in virtual reality before, which isn't unusual—many of my clients have never experienced immersive technology inside a head-mounted display, what we call an HMD. Having read headlines declaring "VR is the future!" and watched videos about the technology being the "ultimate empathy machine," they are intrigued with its potential to tell their existing message in a more resonant way.

This particular project was short on time, so they had preemptively hired a production team consisting of a director, a camera operator, a sound designer, and an editor. What they had done was hire a film crew to tell a story in a virtual reality experience.

Around the same time, I began guest lecturing on virtual reality and augmented reality at Yale University. Undergraduate and graduate students from diverse disciplines—art, architecture, computer science, and drama—attended. Few had hands-on experience with immersive technology, so they approached VR projects similarly to the GoogleVR client: they brought a story or experience they wanted to tell in another medium and wondered: how do I do this, but in VR?

Across hundreds of academic, professional, and creative interactions, I kept coming back to a singular problem. Clients, students, researchers, reviewers, creators and even many of my esteemed colleagues were all in the mindset of trying to tell a story with their immersive experiences.

STORYTELLING IS SUCH A WELL-ESTABLISHED PARADIGM THAT EVEN CONSIDERING THE POSSIBILITY OF DOING SOMETHING OTHER THAN TELLING A STORY WITH TECHNOLOGY SEEMS...

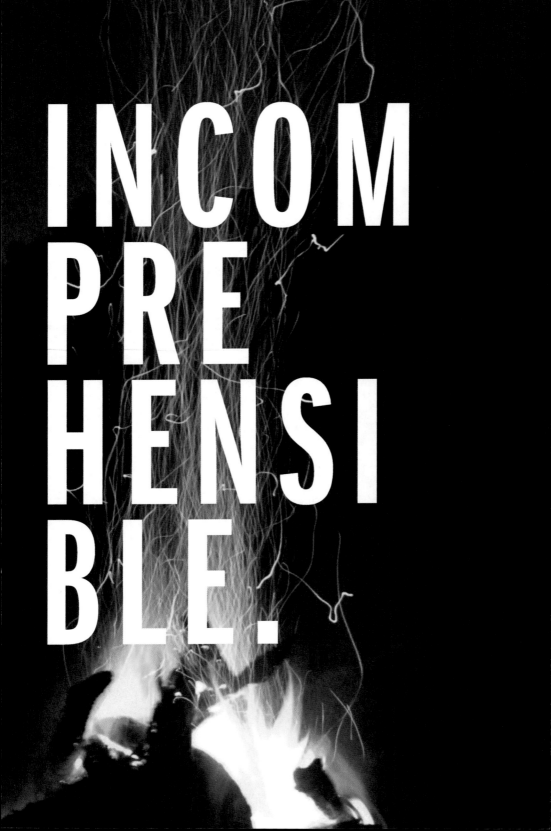

In limestone caves on the majestic Indonesian island of Sulawesi, ancient human hands pressed up against the cold rock face—and stayed there for 40,000 years.

Chaotic smatterings of fingers painted onto the rock face reach out to us from the past, like ghosts trying to escape Dante's purgatory. We have been steadily evolving the symbolic representations of our reality since those first stained cave walls.

SINCE THE BEGINNING OF RECORDED HISTORY, STORIES HAVE CONNECTED US TO OUR HUMANITY, SWAYED OUR OPINIONS, CHANGED OUR BEHAVIOR, BUILT OUR BUSINESSES, AND COLORED OUR EXISTENCE. THEY CONNECT US WITH

THE CORE OF OUR BEING.

EACH transformation IN tools evolves humanity itself.

The ancient Egyptians preserved stories by sketching pictures into stone, then experimented with portable writing surfaces. Local papyrus plants were woven into flat writing surfaces that could be rolled into a scroll. Gluing multiple scrolls together made it possible to record longer stories. More complex stories increased the numbers of pictures to be memorized. Hundreds of symbols expanded into thousands.

Pictographic symbols transformed into alphabets that could be infinitely combined and easily remembered. Writing systems flourished. As those expanded, thought processes abstracted. Philosophical inquiry and academic institutions began to thrive.

Content exploded. Humanity needed an easy way to replicate and distribute books. Printers who once carved entire pages onto blocks of wood embraced the moveable type printing press, which could produce multiple copies of lengthy written works at great speed. Within decades, mass-produced printed books were available across Europe. The price of books dropped and access to information increased, educating the masses and allowing scholars to more readily share ideas.

TECHNOLOGY ALTERS WHAT IS POSSIBLE,

WHICH IN TURN EXPANDS OUR PERCEPTION OF WHAT IS POSSIBLE.

Photographs published in monthly issues of *The Photographic Times* in 1895 were mostly simple portraits and landscapes interspersed with articles describing how to photograph the same.

Topics included the microscopic traits of spiders, the difficulty of photographing children, and the mechanisms of primitive electric lighting. Yet on a wintery evening, in the basement of Le Salon Indien du Grand Café in Paris, spectators gathered to witness the phenomenon of *photographs that moved*. The Lumière brothers projected a series of short 50-second films, mostly showing casual scenes of people walking about. One of the moving images captured a train charging directly at the audience. According to reporters in attendance, everyone in the room "jumped up in shock, as they feared getting run over" and "ran out of the hall in terror because the locomotive headed right for them. They feared that it could plunge off the screen and onto them."

Whether or not these accounts were true, the media was captivated and news of the moving images spread throughout Europe.

Reactions to early virtual reality experiences were similarly dramatic. As soon as HMDs entered household living rooms, reaction videos hit the internet. People strapped into headsets screamed their faces off on virtual rollercoasters, shouted in fear while "falling" off invisible ledges, howled as they guarded themselves against virtual creatures, and ran face-first into real walls while they were full sprint in a virtual world.

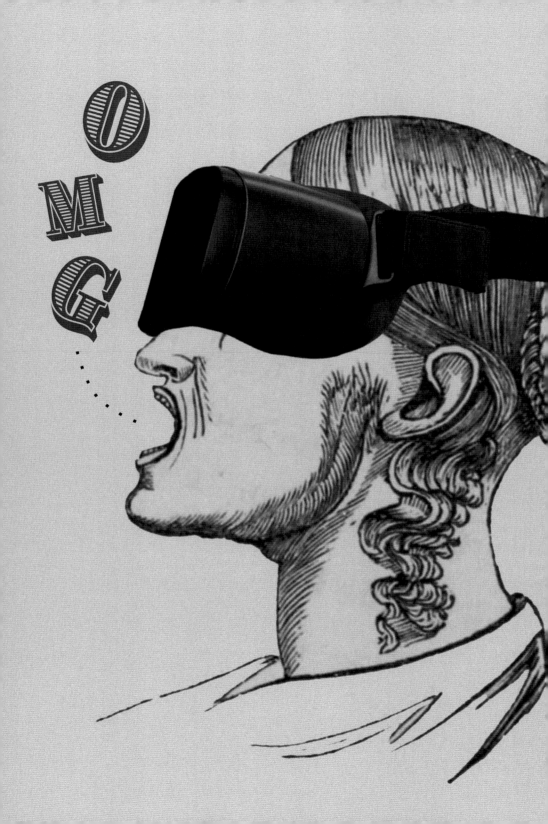

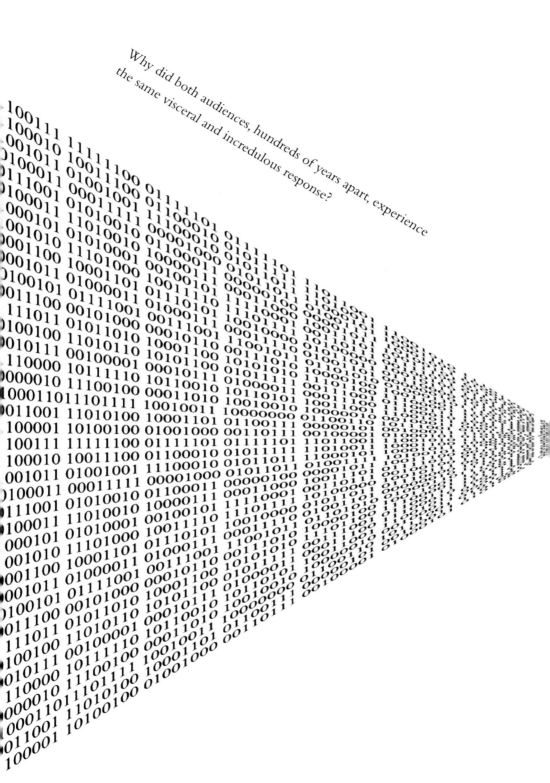

Why did both audiences, hundreds of years apart, experience the same visceral and incredulous response?

The technology defied their expectations of how the world should or did function.

Spectators watching the Lumière brothers' projections lived in a world where images hung quietly on walls and most certainly did not move. Even in flickering black and white with no sound, the sight of a train barreling towards them was spectacular. Likewise, today's creators and audiences live in a world where content is generally contained in frames and stories are, for the most part, told.

As we incorporate computers, interactivity, and agency into our stories, those stories will evolve.

And so will we.

Classical, pre-computational storytelling mediums are restricted by the capabilities of human nature. Our lives progress moment to moment from a singular point of view with irreversible sequences. Likewise, our stories have been expressed one word, one scene, one chapter, one image at a time. Followed by the next. And the next. And the next, in a linear progression of ideas created as a reflection of our own existence. And so we cling to our beloved storytelling, even as technology expands beyond the human capacity for expression. With tools that can now create realms of multiple realities where numerous plotlines exist simultaneously and the digital and real worlds can interact with and influence each other, a new paradigm must emerge that encompasses these new capabilities.

I floated the idea of narrative evolution at one of the Yale lectures, proposing we shift away from the linear constructs of *telling* in order to galvanize the full potential immersive technology. Esteemed professors shook their heads. Students questioned The End of Storytelling as if stories would cease to exist.

"The End" has fascinated storytellers throughout time. Beyond The End is the Unknown, filled with mystical and frightening possibilities—including new beginnings. Ancient civilizations, believing they lived on a flat Earth, told stories about demons living alongside gods beyond the edge of the world. Centuries after the world was known to be round, Washington Irving used the power of story to create the myth that Christopher Columbus risked the lives of himself and his crew sailing off the edge of the earth, only to find a new world. As I began to venture into the uncharted territory of immersive thinking, the "maps" that guided storytellers in their craft began to seem like maps of a flat Earth being used to navigate a spherical world. Established methodologies and familiar phrases limited our ability to expand into the possibilities of a new reality.

FAMILIAR PHRASES

INTERACTIVE STORYTELLING

IMMERSIVE STORYTELLING

IMMERSIVE STORYTELLING IN VR

IMMERSIVE STORYTELLING FOR VR

VR STORYTELLING

DIGITAL STORYTELLING

LET US RELEASE OURSELVES FROM THE CONSTRAINTS OF CENTURIES OF STORY*TELLING*.

IMMERSIVE NARRATIVES INVOLVE A COMPLEX INTERWOVEN NETWORK OF STORY, TECHNOLOGY, AND HUMANITY. THIS IS THE STORYPLEX.

EVALUATE THE TOOLS AT HAND

The tools used to create immersive experiences will be rapidly evolving for the foreseeable future. Rather than explore current hardware and the latest software trends in-depth, it makes more sense to delve into the capabilities and limitations of the wide array of tools currently available. This provides more meaningful context for creating immersive, interactive experiences today and for guiding their future evolution.

THINK AND BUILD DIFFERENTLY

Interactive experiences challenge us to move beyond the art of the "tell." Immersive, computationally in-volved narratives demand a different way of thinking. Expanding our stories beyond traditional storytelling requires us to reconsider the symbols of expression, and evolve how we approach content creation.

UNDERSTAND WHERE WE ARE AND WHAT NEEDS TO CHANGE

Throughout history, stories and technology have been intricately intertwined. Innovations slowly become accepted standards. Standards allow for consistency, predictability and industry development, and with time, those standards become constraints. Constraints chain us to convention; they set patterns of behavior and expectations. When a new technology arises, we must resist the urge to force our established mentality on to it.

ENVISION THE FUTURE

Immersive technology and the worlds we create with them will continue to evolve and expand. While our most epic visions may not be executable yet, we can start to think bigger—both for ourselves and our future.

IMMERSIVE
TECHNOLOGY

CHEATSHEET

WHAT IS IMMERSIVE TECHNOLOGY?

WHEREAS WE WERE once undoubtedly
separated from the content which we created, today's
technology has the potential to replace our sensory
input entirely. Digital assets augment or substitute
real-world simulations, blurring the line between
symbolic representations and the known world. This is
what we call immersive technology, the computerized
integration of digital components with the real world.

In 1994, scholar Paul Milgram attempted to define
the difference between two technologies: virtual reality and augmented reality. To do this, he created the
reality-virtuality continuum. On one end of the spectrum was the real world, the one we naturally interact
with daily. On the opposite end, computing systems
replace the real world completely. In between are

varying degrees of mixed reality, depending on how much the technology replaced the real world. Today, the industry continues to debate the relationship between VR, AR, and MR technologies according to Milgrim's spectrum. Meanwhile, our relationship to content in immersive technology has begun to evolve. How far a technology takes us away from reality is an academic contemplation. What is increasingly important in understanding the practical application of these technologies is *how they integrate content with reality.*

Technology that represents but does not integrate with the real world is all around us—in photographs, films, books, and paintings, for example. These traditional mediums are what I call Classical Realism. Replacing sensory input by mapping it to digital content only produces partially-integrated Virtual Reality experiences. Visually immersive HMDs or physically responsive haptic devices used in VR experiences lack the ability to account for and incorporate input from the physical world—they only replace it. However, Enhanced Reality technologies integrate properties from real world elements with digital assets to create highly-integrated content. These include today's augmented reality and mixed reality industries. As we move from defining technology to integrating it into our stories and our lives, here's a quick overview of how it all comes together—in the year 2019.

THE STORYPLEX
SPECTRUM...

REALITY

CLASSICAL
REALISM

REAL ENVIRONMENT

PHOTOGRAPHY
VIDEO

VIRTUAL REALITY

ENHANCED REALITY

360
SPATIAL
INTERACTIVE

AUGMENTED REALITY
MIXED REALITY
AUGMENTED VIRTUALITY
INTEGRATED REALITY

Tucked away on the western shoreline of Costa Rica rests the peaceful town of Manuel Antonio. From a particularly high hill on the outskirts of town, you can look down across crisp white beaches curving around an inlet of deep blue ocean waters. It is a dramatic view. Directly behind you are the towering trees of a dense rainforest growing right up to the edge of the hill.

Close your eyes for a second and envision the real world scene I describe. Do you have it pictured in your mind? Do you think it's similar to the one I experienced?

■ ■ ■ ■ ■   ■ ■ ■ ■ ■   ■ ■ ■ ■   ■ ■ ■   ■ ■

Likely, your brain interpreted my words to construct a scene based on your own experiences. The color of the ocean, the density of the rainforest, and the height of the hill are subject to your interpretation of my words. How high is "high?" What color is "deep blue?"

To see how similar my beach is to your imagined beach, let's say I show you a photograph from the exact location on the hill where I stood. The picture would show the landscape described, with even more precision. The beach in my photo might be slightly narrower than the one you imagined, or perhaps the trees in the rainforest differ in height and density. Still, that picture would only show us a small fraction of the view. To see the entire panorama from the beach overlook around to the forest in the opposite direction, I would need to show you a series of pictures or a panoramic photograph. Now we have the entire scene, although only along a horizontal axis and just for one moment in time. What about the movement of the waves? How quietly did they lap against the beach?

■

To extend that moment, I share a video taken from the same spot. You see the grouping of the waves and hear the gentle sound of their crashes into the sand from the distance. Our shared visions of this idyllic beach are starting to align. Still, the traditional video only shows a window into a small section of the scene. If monkeys start playing in the trees behind the video while the camera is pointed towards the ocean, you wouldn't be able to see them.

■ ■ ■ ■ ■ ■   ■ ■ ■ ■ ■   ■ ■ ■ ■   ■ ■ ■   ■ ■

You are probably familiar with the photographic and video technology we've shared thus far that allows us to capture and share windows of information. Now, let's get immersive.

VIRTUAL REALITY: 360

On the same hillside in Costa Rica, let's say I film the scene with a camera that records all directions simultaneously. The edges of the frame disappear, capturing a spherical image so that when you view it, you can look in any direction at any moment you choose. When the monkeys hoot and howl behind you, you can turn around to look because they have been filmed simultaneously with the beach-side overlook. If you look up, you see the cloudless blue sky. This is called 360 content and can be captured as an image or video.

■ ■ ■

360 content is created by capturing footage from multiple angles simultaneously. Because these recordings are done from a singular position (that of the camera), people viewing the 360 content are not able to move and navigate within the environment.

■

Let's take that even further and say that while being surrounded by the scene at Manuel Antonio in a 360 experience, you could then walk along the dramatic hillside edge
within the scene. You step over tree roots, careful not to
trip and lose your balance. The severe height of the ledge
might give you vertigo, causing you to step back towards
the trees and instead go find the monkeys calling from the
canopy. This is a spatial virtual reality experience, where
you can navigate through a digital environment.

■ ■ ■

Navigating spatial VR experiences is often done with input
from an HMD, called "head tracking," or from controllers
held in the hand or placed on the body. Some experiences
have custom hardware built that guests can navigate with,
such as the VR flight simulator Birdly® where guests mount
an apparatus that allows them to move their arms and
legs to control their flight path.

■

As you walk into the simulated rainforest, you come across a banana and reach down to coax the hidden monkeys out of the trees. One of the fearless Costa Rican animals is tempted by your offer and aggressively scurries towards you. Not wanting to chance a primal encounter, you throw the banana, scaring him back into the forest. You just interacted with an environmental object in a manner that affects other elements in the scene. This is an interactive, immersive virtual reality experience.

■ ■ ■

Spatial and Interactive virtual environments are typically created with software called a "game engine." This software contains the code for core interactive functionality, freeing up developers to integrate creative assets into the experience.

■ ■ ■ ■ ■ ■ ■ ■ ■ ■ ■ ■ ■ ■ ■ ■ ■ ■ ■

Up to this point, each of these immersive examples transported you to Manuel Antonio. Let's say we want to integrate components of the Costa Rican beach back into the real world.

ENHANCED REALITY: AUGMENTED REALITY

Back in Manhattan, we create a 3D model of the monkey and name it Bobo. We upload animations of Bobo to a mobile app that are triggered by physical markers placed around the city. When people hold a smartphone up to the markers, the 3D model of Bobo appears, overlaid onto the real world. Our application, which augments the real world with digital content, is an augmented reality experience.

■ ■ ■

In an AR system, guests see digital content overlaid onto real-world environments but the content does not interact with the real world. Google Glass was an early AR device. Since then, companies use the camera lens on mobile devices as a pass-through viewing mechanism over which digital content is layered. Businesses are utilizing AR for a wide range of applications from product visualization to remote collaboration, training, and tourism.

If the computer in our office is connected to a controller with motion sensing capability, we can interact with Bobo. In the virtual world, we can make the controller appear as a banana that Bobo hungrily follows as we move the controller. When we "throw" the banana, he jumps up to catch and eat it. The ability to interact with digital content that responds to real-world actions is augmented virtuality.

■ ■ ■

Gaming consoles have provided AV experiences for over a decade. In 2006, the Nintendo Wii console shipped with a hand-held remote with spatial motion-tracking. As a player physically moved the Wii remote around a room, they interacted with virtual objects in the game. Players could ace a tennis serve, roll a bowling ball, or swing a golf club simply by moving the remote. The revolutionary and fun AV-based interaction technique made *Wii Sports* the best-selling game of all time for a single platform.

ENHANCED REALITY: MIXED REALITY

Up to this point, Bobo has been able to interact with guest input independently from the real world. Certain HMDs allow the wearer to see both the physical environment and digital projections, and can track guest actions as well as map objects in the real world for our digital Bobo to interact and respond to. Using this technology, Bobo can now hide behind physical desks and jump up on real chairs to demand a banana. When digital content responds to elements in a real environment, that is mixed reality.

■ ■ ■

Mixed Reality has confusingly been used to describe various styles of interaction. Today, it most commonly refers to when the guest can simultaneously see the real world and digital content, and that content registers and responds to real-world information. Unlike AR and AV, in MR, the real world is mapped into the experience and becomes part of the interactions.

Let's say we now build an installation where objects in physical space map to a virtual environment. For example, a series of tall white cylinders stand in an empty room. Once we put our HMD on, the cylinders are digitally represented as tree trunks in a luscious jungle. When we reach out in the real world, we physically feel the cylindrical tree trunks that Bob is climbing to the top of the virtual canopy. This is integrated reality.

■ ■ ■

Integrated reality aligns the presence of physical "sets" or haptic input devices with the sensory effects experienced in the HMD. These haptic affordances facilitate the illusion of being physically present in a virtual environment. A company called The Void has been successful in creating these IR experiences for *Star Wars* and *Ghostbusters*.

Integrated Reality experiences are not limited to those built for an HMD. Live action experiences such as location-based entertainment, immersive theatre performances and escape rooms occur in the real-world and use immersive technology to create integrated reality that can sometimes be even more powerful than their virtual world counterparts.

WALKING THROUGH virtual rainforests of Costa Rica or playing with an interactive Bobo who bounces around the office are vastly different experiences than passively looking at a still photograph or video. Immersive technologies invite us into experiences and surround us with environments, integrating digital encounters with our physical reality. As the line between real and digital blurs with increasingly sophisticated technology, so will the lines between the technologies on the Storyplex spectrum.

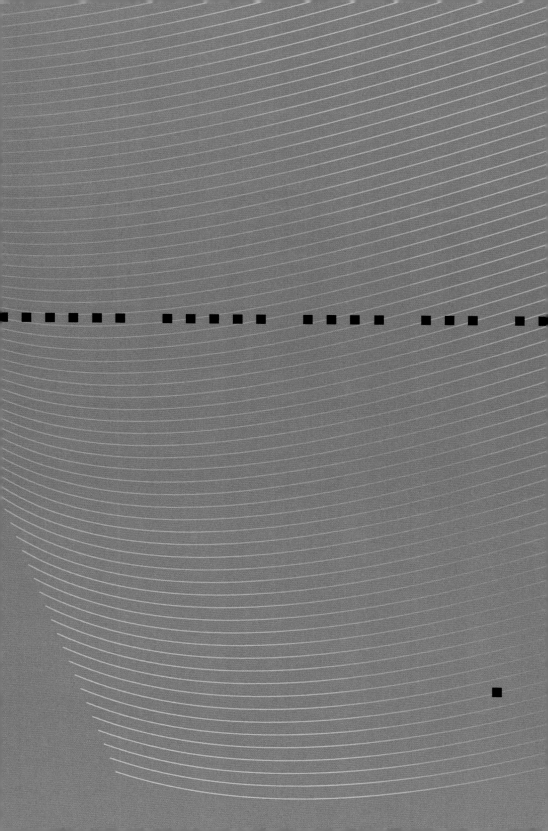

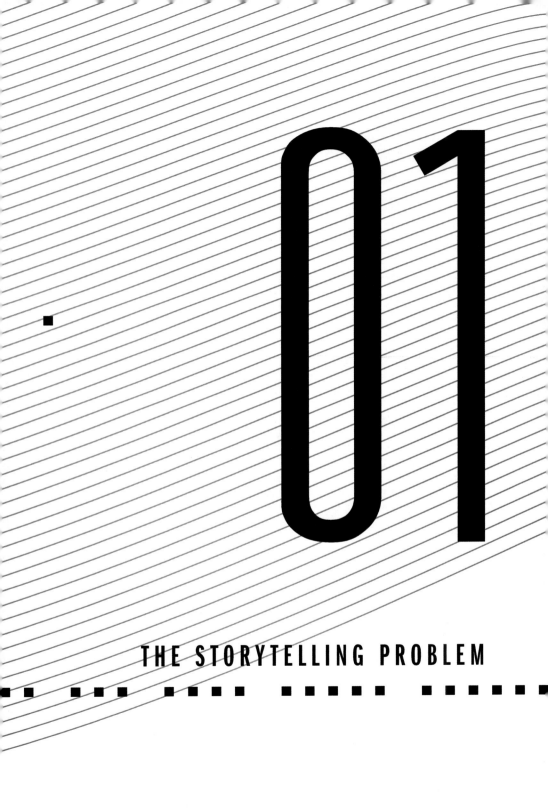

01

THE STORYTELLING PROBLEM

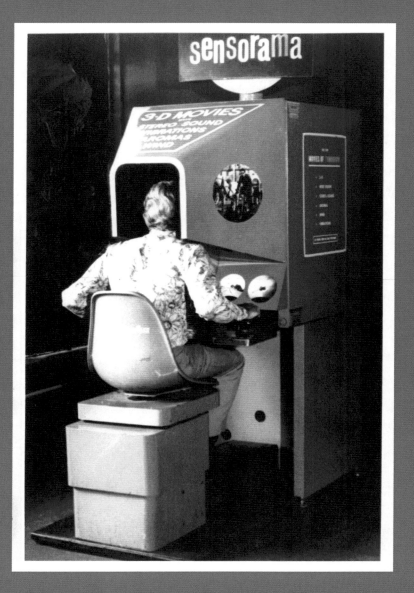

GROWING UP IN A SMALL HOUSE with a dad who worked from home meant that my younger brother and I were not allowed to stay inside and raise the usual ruckus during summer break. No television. No video games. We had to venture out into the vast, unexplored depths of the state park behind our house. The banks of the Chattahoochee River were our playground and curious creatures of the woods were our companions. We would venture out to the forest and into worlds that only existed in our minds. As with many people's childhoods, the vast unknown land of make-believe was my first encounter with virtual reality.

As my brother and I ran into the scorching 100-degree sun, the screen door slamming behind us, we dashed across what seemed like miles of manicured lawn to reach a wall of soaring Georgia pines. To me, the edge of the woods that towered above us wasn't made of trees at all. It was an entrance to a fortress. We scaled the "stone walls" on dangerous ladders imagined out of thin branches that would break and send us tumbling to the ground. Having conquered the stone barrier, we leapt to the ground, only to find ourselves surrounded by swarms of soldiering ants marching towards victory—unless we defeat them! Our imaginations shrunk us down so that we might see our enemy eye-to-eye. Quick! Build the barricades! Gather the troops and halt their advance! Twigs sprung to our defense, piling up to reroute the poor creatures unknowingly intruding on our asylum. The perimeter secured, onward we went, following non-existent paths into places far away from objective reality.

When structured activities replaced impromptu backyard conquests, the theatre became my playground. My spiral-bound notebooks were littered with stick-figure sketches of choreography for community plays. On gridded paper I etched out scenic sets for our high school productions. What I didn't realize was that, in the process of adapting my imaginary worlds to an established medium, my imagination was being slowly chained to convention. The interactive stories that I explored freely as a child gave way to pre-scripted dramas delegated to the confines of a stage for an audience.

The conflict between creating stories in the freedom of the forests and crafting them for an established medium would come to the fore in a Set Design 101 class at Carnegie Mellon University. One particular design project required us to select a story, design the set, and construct it on a 1/4 scale with thin pieces of cut-out cardboard. The set I imagined was the expansive rainforest of *The Jungle Book*. Massive trees extended to the sky and branches reached across the middle of the performance space, creating shadows where characters would lurk. Never once did I imagine the production being behind a proscenium arch. I envisioned the audience walking around the jungle, climbing the trees for different vantage points and exploring the parts and characters of the story that they found interesting.

It didn't go over very well. My design conflicted with the realities of producing modern theatre. First, there are the physical playhouses: traditional theatres seat their audiences in rows of seats facing a stage. And then there's the narrative structure of plays.

Playwrights script their stories in the centuries-old tradition of entrances and exits onto stage. There was also the problem of audience expectations. How could I possibly tell the story of Mowgli's adventures with Baloo and Bagheera when the audience, free to roam through the space, may miss any given part of the story at any time? These were fair critiques from the faculty, given the practicalities of the theatre industry. To me, however, the story felt trapped in the proscenium and strangled by convention.

A fortunate disaster helped me return to the forest.

Graduation requirements for all majors at Carnegie Mellon included learning how to code a website from scratch. Even theatre majors had to pass a course where we hard-coded an HTML page. Now, this was in the '90s and at the time I thought of computers as glorified typewriters for high-school keyboarding classes. How computers functioned was a complete mystery to me; I didn't discover what "email" was until I set foot on the university campus straight out of a Georgia public high school. I had to ask other students what the difference between a "PC" and a "Mac" was, and was further confused by the answer. Why was one called a "personal computer" when technically both were personal computers? So the concept of code was mind-blowing to say the least. Having to learn to write it felt like an exercise in torture. I failed my first computer basics class.

As I hacked away at both my fears of the unknown and HTML code, I realized that what I was building allowed multiple realities to exist at the same time. In a computer program, a series of events could be experienced linearly while the code running on the backend allowed for any number of interactions to occur. In my narrative mind, this meant multiple stories co-existed within the code while the choices of the user determined which story they followed. I was going to have to dig deeper than basic website design if I wanted to figure out how to make the code do what I wanted it to do for stories, though. One specific area of study in the School of Computer Science interested me: Human-Computer Interaction. HCI integrated psychology and design with computer science. By studying how users interact with computer systems, we could make design choices to influence and improve the experience. The coursework focused on designing interfaces for technologies such as Palm Pilots, but it fascinated me as a way to create narratives. A year after failing that first class, I was in the Dean's office convincing him to let me double major in Computer Science.

One particular course brought together my seemingly disparate worlds of story and computing: Building Virtual Worlds. Launched by the legendary computer science professor Randy Pausch at a time where few people had HMDs or computers even powerful enough to run them, this interdisciplinary class brought together engineers, designers, artists, architects and theatre students. Every two weeks students would form new groups of four who would ideate, implement, test, and demo an interactive virtual world from scratch. Sometimes concepts worked, and sometimes the builds failed to even run. The rapid iteration process in BVW was a way of keeping any one idea from becoming too precious, but it was also incredibly demanding. I slept under computers in the lab while code compiled and then would run to directing class with the theatre students when the sun came up. The next year, I was invited to join Randy's newly launched Masters of Entertainment Technology program as an undergraduate. Through the program's expansive mission to combine the worlds of art and technology, I continued exploring the intersection of storytelling and technology in unexpectedly fascinating ways: codifying personality algorithms for autonomous robots using Commedia dell'Arte and researching location-based immersive entertainment experiences.

I share this story for three reasons. First, my background was in theatre and my youth was largely void of electronics. I had extremely limited exposure to computers or coding when I entered college. I empathize with everyone for whom the language of computing seems terrifying. But it is possible — and even necessary — to push through those fears to embrace the capabilities of immersive, interactive technology. Secondly, the stories we imagine as children aren't confined to broadcast-ready specifications. They aren't contained in a 4k rectangular screen or encountered as a passive experience. That childlike sense of diving into an evolving, responsive environment is at the core of immersive experiences. Which leads to my third reason: Centuries of storytelling has conditioned how we approach narratives, but new tools change what's possible to imagine and create.

Early computers could only perform simple calculations. As they grew in sophistication and speed, computers became an extension of other human skills, allowing us to do what we had previously done, but faster and more precisely. Inevitably, their capabilities expanded into the realm of supporting creative expression and providing entertainment. It would seem logical that the way we've told stories with other technologies would also work in this new medium. But three fundamental traits of immersive experiences undermine the traditional process of *telling* stories:

ABSENCE OF FRAME
SENSATION OF PRESENCE
RESPONSIVE SCRIPTING

ABSENCE OF FRAME

As you read this book, you are flipping through page after page of words. Or perhaps you are scrolling through an electronic version of pages on your tablet. Let's say you are reading this in the morning, in a little while you will head to work where you sit at your desk and sort through emails on your computer before finishing a presentation to your team on how to incorporate VR into your business strategy. During the work day, you might check your text messages on your phone. And after you return home you turn on the television to catch up on the local news while browsing your favorite social media applications on your laptop. A friend messages you to make plans to see the latest movie, but the screening times conflict with when you have plans to go on a hike to take pictures of a nearby nature preserve with your new DSLR camera.

Think about each of the devices just mentioned: book, tablet, computer, projector, mobile phone, television, laptop, website, film, camera. What do they have in common? A framed rectangular interface.

The frame is so ubiquitous that we rarely notice it. But once you start seeing it, it's everywhere. Billboards. ATMs. Menus at restaurants. *The frame separates pre-scripted content from our naturally interactive reality.* It's no wonder that when someone over the age of twenty puts on an HMD to experience immersive technology for the first time, they sit down and look straight ahead without turning their heads. That's what framed content has trained us to do!

In fact, each form of story*telling* has a frame, even spoken words.

Written Frames

The frame in your hands right now evolved over tens of thousands of years. The shape of the paper in this book has been standardized for mass reproduction and distribution. The size fits easily in your hands, and the length is short enough to make it conveniently transportable and, hopefully, shareable. We're dealing with frames whether we are writing letters home, posting on a blog, reading the newspaper, or projecting a presentation in a conference room. They are so ubiquitous that our minds no longer take notice of the visual constraint. Instead, we have conditioned ourselves to extract meaning from areas designated to contain content. We are not thinking about Egyptian papyrus rolls as we turn pages through epic adventures at Hogwarts or negotiate the details of billion-dollar business contracts. The paradigm of the framed, written word is fundamentally ingrained in almost every form of written communication.

Oral Frames

In Ancient Greece, groups of male performers sung hymns called dithyrambs in honor of Dionysus. Together they created a chorus that performed characters in unison. As legend goes, one day during a Festival, as dithyrambs were being sung, a performer named Thespis sprung out from the chorus and began reciting the chorus lines as if he were the character. This ushered in a new era of drama wherein actors embodied their characters. Today we call performers "thespians" in honor of the first actor.

Theatrical productions adapted to embrace this new form of expression. Circular dithyrambic celebrations shifted to having a performance area with the audience seated in a semi-circle on a natural hill for optimal viewing and acoustics. A tent was placed behind the performance area to provide a place for the actors to change costumes, while also creatively doubling as background scenery. The original Greek name for the tent was *skene*. In front of the skene was the *prosk nion*, which literally means "before the stage." Here the chorus and actors performed their shows. The raised *proscenium* platform evolved to also have a physical proscenium arch which served to frame the action on stage and consolidate the audience's attention to a single area. The proscenium arch continues to frame live performances in theatres, concert halls, and opera houses around the world today.

Aural Frames

Audio recordings and broadcasts have been framed by the technology transmitting the sound. From the horn of a phonograph to the electrodynamic loudspeaker, devices provide sound from the specific direction of the speaker. President Franklin D. Roosevelt's fireside chats in the late 1930s and early 1940s entered American homes through wooden console radios. Movie theatre sound technology progressively pushed the boundaries of the frame from a live organist vamping sounds for silent films to monophonic systems with one speaker, then stereophonic with two speakers, and now the Dolby systems create "surround sound." Still, the speakers provide a directional reference point from which artificially created sound emanates.

Visual Frames

Creators in visual disciplines often work within a framed environment as well. The canvas provides a frame for the painter. Printmakers apply their craft to paper. Ancient "drawings with light" made by observing the light projected onto the opposite wall through a small hole evolved into today's photography industry. Composing a shot within a frame has become an artform in still photos as well as motion pictures. The frame limits the audience's field of view to focus their attention at what the director wants them to see.

To previsualize the action in film frame, directors storyboard sketches in a series of rectangles. These framed drawings indicate information such as where the camera and actors should be placed, what the focus of the shot is, how the lighting and scenery are arranged within the frame, and how the camera frame moves. Famed film director and master of suspense Alfred Hitchcock notably used storyboard sketches to both plan for shots and brainstorm solutions. Framing what the audience saw and when they saw it allowed Hitchcock to craft powerfully suspenseful sequences.

Digital Frames

Out of cinema came "Motion Pictures by Wireless," where visual content was broadcast to remote locations, which we now call "television." As the television industry boomed and TV sets were installed in homes across America, the movie industry made a bold move to compete: they changed the size of the frame. Originally both film and television were filmed and displayed in a 4x3 rectangle. The film industry then changed its aspect ratio to 16x9 to differentiate themselves, which is why we now have "widescreen" formats. Then analog television gave way to higher-definition television. Now many of us watch what was once television content on computer screens and TVs are output devices for video game consoles.

Advancements in technology allowed more information to be stored on smaller devices. Both computing machines and display frames became increasingly portable, inexpensive, and higher quality (are you recognizing a pattern of technological evolution here?) until handheld rectangles could fit in our pockets as today's smartphones. But the frame persisted.

Constraints of the Frame

Frames create both physical and mental constraints. How we frame a story, frame a concept, or frame a situation has the power to change how we view that information. Removing the frame not only alters the content; it also dramatically changes our *relationship to* the content.

IF THE CONCEPT OF A "FRAME" IS BOTH A STRUCTURAL AND MENTAL CONSTRAINT, WHAT HAPPENS WHEN IT IS TAKEN AWAY?

■ ■ ■ ■ ■　■ ■ ■ ■　■ ■ ■　■ ■　　　■

PATTERNS APPEAR IN
PLACE OF STRUCTURES.

The symmetry of snowflakes, fractal branching of trees, or flow of energy waves all expand naturally beyond rectilinear frames. And so does humanity. No one asks, "Where am I supposed to look?" as they navigate the streets of New York City or swim along the Great Barrier Reef. When there is no frame, we look where we please, act on what we are compelled to respond to, and respond to our environment as it, in turn, responds to us.

WE EXPERIENCE.

SENSATION OF PRESENCE

In 2015, I met with a small business owner who was interested in using VR as a sales tool for his team to convert potential clients into buyers. He wasn't familiar with virtual reality other than the splashy headlines about it being a technology that could make people feel as if they were somewhere else. His existing sales method involved demonstrating an environmental product that could only be cultivated in a remote location in the middle of the Atlantic Ocean. Bringing potential clients to this location required multiple plane trips, rickety bus rides, and helicopter flights out across the ocean. It was a financially exhaustive and time-consuming journey that turned many would-be buyers off. And the cost of transporting even the few executives who wanted to take this long trip was draining his business. Yet, he said, when executives did come out, they immediately realized how unique his product was, resulting in an almost 100 percent sales conversion. What if he could transport them to the ocean without the physical journey? What if he could remotely connect each potential client emotionally and viscerally to his unique factory? And then what if he could duplicate that at minimal cost and distribute it around the world? It would save money, increase his exposure, and reduce the carbon footprint of his environmentally-aware organization.

He had already tried filming the location with a traditional camera and putting the footage in presentations for his sales staff to take to potential clients, but it wasn't commanding any new business. We talked through the advantages and disadvantages of the immersive technologies available. Not ready to take on the expense of creating a spatial or interactive experience, he opted to create a 360 video.

Initially he proposed replicating the same content he had filmed in a documentary-style video trailer—only in 360. Instead, I had him set his prepared script aside, and we discussed the experience that he wanted his potential clients to have. He wanted them to feel the exclusivity of the location and soar over the expansive ocean waters. These conversations dramatically restructured the concept, reduced dialogue-heavy descriptions and eliminated film-style shots that he had assumed would be usable. Instead we built in audience-directed moments, designed smooth scene transitions, and crafted moments that would be unforgettable to experience.

The final experience was loaded onto mobile VR devices and distributed to his sales team. Now his team was able to bring the ocean to their clients. The results were impressive. The simple 360 video immersive experience had an almost 100 percent conversion rate while expanding the reach of the sales team and eliminating the costs of traveling dozens of reluctant executives around the world.

The same company was represented in both the traditional video and the 360 experience. What was the difference?

Mobile VR wasn't readily available at the time, which certainly aligned his brand with cutting-edge technology. But his success was more due to evolving his content from being something told to something that was experienced. Inside the headset, the clients felt present in the location. Free from distractions, they were also free to physically turn their heads and look at was important to their decision-making process. They experienced the real-world magnitude of his operation, felt the dramatic effects of its remoteness, and trusted a 360 field of view where nothing was hidden from view.

Immersion

The first time I heard the overture to Richard Wagner's epic opera *Tannhauser*, I was researching Wagner's philosophy of Gesamtkunstwerk, or "total work of art." Having come across a copy of Tannhauser at my local library, I took it home and inserted it into a CD player,not knowing what to expect. The sleepy opening of the overture drizzled out of the speakers; the strings methodically layered in, stretching out the melody until the brass joined, pushing the theme forward as the strings receded, swirling underneath the pulsating melody. I sat transfixed, the instruments delicately balancing, fiercely surging, gracefully falling back, through to its triumphant finale. Without even knowing the plot of *Tannhauser*, the orchestration had swept me away on a dramatic mythological romance. For those 15 minutes I was completely immersed in the soaring, scaling spectacle of Wagner's musical fantasy.

Janet Murray, professor in the School of Literature, Media, and Communication at the Georgia Institute of Technology, and author of *Hamlet on the Holodeck*, described the quality of immersion as when "we seek the same feeling from a psychologically immersive experience that we do from a plunge in the ocean or swimming pool: the sensation of being surrounded by a completely other reality." Immersion is the mental representation of a virtual space, a transportation to an altered mental state. To continue with Murray's analogy, the moment you submerge yourself into a body of water, everything that you know to be real on terrestrial ground alters. Your hearing deafens, your weight lightens, your sight blurs. Even the sunlight bends and refracts. Whether you are immersed in a physical pool of water or learning a new language, the reality you previously experienced gives way to a new sensory experience.

The film industry has frequently used advancements in technology to increasingly immerse audiences. Visually, the industry has progressed the image from black and white to color, widened and multiplied the number of screens in the theatre, and created depth through 3D glasses. Aurally, silent films accompanied by live organ players eventually incorporated simultaneous soundtracks, and theater speakers have evolved from monosound to multi-directional stereophonic systems.

Inspired by the myriad of cinematic developments, an unknown cinematographer, Morton Heilig, envisioned combining all of the sensory elements together to create "The Cinema of the Future." In his pitch documents, he commanded, "Open your eyes, listen, smell, and feel—sense the world in all its magnificent colors, depth, sounds, odors, and textures—this is the cinema of the future! The screen will not fill only 5 percent of your visual field as the local movie screen does, or the mere 7.5 percent of Wide Screen, or 18 percent of the 'miracle mirror' screen of Cinemascope, or the 25 percent of Cinerama—but 100 percent."

Heilig claimed his visionary Sensorama device would create an experience "so life-like that it gives the spectator the sensation of being *physically* in the scene," engaging not just his body, but his soul. His impassioned manifesto failed to attract investors. It would be another decade until he was able to finance a prototype build of the Sensorama, which is largely regarded to be the first working virtual reality machine.

Heilig hypothesized that sight was only 70% of a person's sensory experience. To create the Cinema of the Future, the wide-angle 3D images in the Sensorama were supplemented by stereo sound, wind fans, scent tracks, and a motion chair. More than a motion picture, he intended to create "the first art form…to reveal the new scientific world to man in the full sensual vividness and dynamic vitality of his consciousness." What Heilig was tapping into was the fact that any medium that so completely envelops our senses such that the world as we know it drops away creates a sense of immersion.

In classical storytelling, such as Wagnerian operas, the audience's imagination constructs a sensation of immersion, whereas immersive technology emits physical stimuli that we psychologically interpret as presence.

Effects of Immersion

An immersive environment doesn't have to be realistic or even follow the rules of terrestrial physics in order to have a profound psychological effect.

A 1998 study by German researchers Regenbrecht, Schubert, & Friedman described the differences between how our brains process increasingly sensorial mediums:

"When we read an article about a narrow suspension bridge, we would rarely experience any sensations because of the mentioned height, but we have a clear mental model of the described space. When we see the bridge in an action movie and we look down to the bottom of the valley together with the endangered protagonist, it is likely that we feel fear because of the height. However, when users have to walk over that bridge in a virtual environment, many of them will experience physiological symptoms and sensations of fear, because they have a sense of actually being there."

■ ■ ■

In 2016, John Patrick Pullen, a *Time* magazine writer reluctant to be wooed by virtual reality, played the VR experience *ToyBox* at a convention. *ToyBox* places two people in a virtual sandbox filled with toys they can interact with. What Pullen described when his "playmate," Erin, shot him with a shrink ray captures the psychological effects of immersion:

"Suddenly, not only were all the toys enormous to me, but Erin's avatar was looming over me like a hulking giant. Her voice even changed as it poured through my headphones, entering my head with a deep, slow tone. And for a moment, I was a child again, with this giant person lovingly playing with me. It gave me such a profound perspective on what it must be like to be my [18-month-old] son, that I started to cry inside the headset. It was a pure and beautiful experience that will reshape my relationship with him moving forward."

■ ■ ■

Chris Klock was an undergraduate student at the Georgia Institute of Technology in 1995 with a debilitating fear of heights. Through a series of VR exposure therapy treatments, he managed to ride in a glass elevator up 49 floors of a building over a visible atrium and look out from a 20-story balcony—in virtual reality. That the environments were cartoonish didn't seem to affect their effectiveness. "In the back of my mind I knew it wasn't real, but I felt I was on the edge of the ledge," Klock recalled. "Even though it looks like an animated reality, all the depth and movement cues are realistic, so it feels real."

Klock was amongst twelve subjects in the first controlled study of VR as a tool for exposure therapy. All were considered to be successfully treated for fear of heights. Similar VR exposure therapies in the mid-90s relieved the fear of flying and PTSD.

Dr. Barbara Rothbaum, who led the studies at Emory University elaborated to the *New York Times*, "for these people to have gotten better, they have to have experienced what computer scientists call a sense of presence." When asked how virtual experiences compared to real-world in exposure therapy treatments, she explained, "You get the same physiological changes—the racing heart, the sweat—that you would in the actual place."

■ ■ ■

Two groups of subjects in a Swiss experiment were asked to place their hands on a table and not move them. They then watched an interactive computer game being played wherein two virtual arms intercepted virtual balls rolling towards the viewer. One group was instructed to simply observe the movements of the two virtual arms. The other group was instructed to observe and *imagine* that the arms were their own. After 84 seconds, the right virtual arm was unexpectedly "stabbed" by a knife and began "bleeding." Both groups responded adversely to being "stabbed," but the observe-and-imagine group showed a significantly higher skin conductance than the observation-only group, a sign of physiological arousal.

The way the brain internalizes and processes stimuli creates its own "virtual reality." The strength of perception in virtual environments is such that the brain overrides objective, intellectual truth—in this case, watching a virtual arm bleed while the participant's arm is not bleeding—to the point of replacing it with meanings it has derived from visual stimuli.

■ ■ ■

In her 1992 paper, Carrie Heeter at MIT defined three dimensions of presence in virtual environments.

"Personal presence" is established when the guest perceives that they physically exist within a virtual world (the Swiss stabbing arm).

"Social presence" occurs through interactions with others in a virtual world (Pullen's *Toy Box* experience).

"Environmental presence" is achieved when the virtual world responds to the guest's presence and interactions (Klock's elevator taking him to the 49th floor).

RESPONSIVE SCRIPTING

"If you're trying to tell a story, you don't want the audience deciding where it should go, that's why you have a director and producer." In saying this, Bran Ferren, the former head of R&D at Walt Disney Imagineering, nailed the primary reason why immersive creators must evolve past the mentality of storytelling: the "telling" of a story delivers a controlled sequence to a passive audience. In immersive mediums, the audience may affect what they see, where they go, or how events transpire in a way that is outside of a storyteller's control. The conflict between "telling" and "experiencing" goes back to the origins of classical and computational mediums.

Scripting: Classical versus Computational

Technology for classical storytelling developed through tools predominantly designed to advance the transmission of ideas. Rolls of papyrus allowed information to be shared with someone who wasn't in the same room as you. The proscenium arch focused an audience's attention, increasing the odds individual audience members would leave with similar impressions of the playwright's words and intentions.

By contrast, computing is an inherently interactive technology. The first computing device, Charles Babbage's Difference Engine, required input from a human in order to function. As computer functions became more complex, new interfaces expanded our ability to interact with the devices: punchcards, keyboards, screens, tracking balls, gamepads; even Heilig's Sensorama and Sutherland's Sword of Damocles were experiential interfaces for an interactive medium. The purpose of these technologies was never to "tell" a story, but to create novel sensory interactions between humans and machines.

Today's digital-native content is centered around interactivity. Video games support multi-player functionality, allowing players around the world to talk, play, and strategize together. Experiences can be broadcast live around the world for strangers to comment and react in real-time. Meanwhile, storytellers grapple with conveying a singular artistic vision in these interactive mediums. This struggle is not new.

Authors have tried to break away from the linear nature of writing for decades. In 1930, Doris Webster and Mary Alden published a branching narrative gamebook called *Consider the Consequences!* The story contained diverging plotlines. A reader chose which story path to follow by turning to pages correlated to their decision on what action a character should take. These precursors to the popular *Choose-Your-Own-Adventure* series alternated between pages of narrative and moments of choice. Ayn Rand's 1934 play, *Night of January 16th*, experimented with multiple endings in a theatrical setting. Set in a courtroom where a secretary is on trial for the murder of her employer, the audience is asked to determine whether she is guilty after hearing both sides of the case. These branching narratives still contain predetermined, pre-scripted plotlines. When my high school drama club produced Rand's play, we rehearsed both potential endings. Each night, one of the two endings was performed. Regardless of what verdict returned from the audience, the resulting ending had been prepared by the production team, ready to play out.

Early game designers followed a similar pattern of alternating between narrative and interaction. Players of Scott Adams's 1978 computer game *Adventureland* input predetermined text commands to move their character through a treasure hunt collecting artifacts. Around the same time, a team from MIT built a more narratively-complex game called *Zork* where players try to stay alive while collecting treasures in an ancient empire. While interactive fiction games can have multiple endings, there is still a linear, predetermined progression of events the audience must follow, all of which lead to pre-established outcomes. Similar actions and results can be seen in immersive theatre, mobile apps, video games, and even interactive films where the audience chooses an action such as "go through the door" or "walk away."

When the first line of a computer program is written, global rules of the world are defined. At this moment, anything is possible. Up could be down. Red could be blue. The empty world is like an author's blank page or painter's empty canvas.

To understand the characteristics of classical storytelling versus computational narratives, let's compare a scene from the iconic Broadway musical *A Chorus Line* being staged for live theatre versus being developed in an interactive game engine. In the signature number "One (Singular Sensation)," nineteen characters of different age, height, ethnicity, and gender, are each wearing spar-kling gold costumes as they move across the stage, singing and high-kicking in unison.

To create the staged performance, the theatre director hires nineteen performers based on a variety of attributes, including vocal range, dance skill, and height. The musical director works with the performers on the vocal arrangement, and a choreographer stages the performers movements during the song. They rehearse, rehearse, and rehearse. The costumes arrive, the lighting cues are set, and the set is constructed. For our theatrical performance, the actors display the artistic confluence onstage in front of an audience.

To create a computationally-based performance of "One" we might build the same scene in a game engine designed for creating interactive 3D virtual experiences. The engine organizes data around "objects" and their attributes. We might start by creating an object. Let's call that object "Performer" and assign it attributes such as age, height, and costume. We then duplicate the object eighteen more times. In each instantiation of the object, we might vary the attributes so that, for example, Performer1 is taller than Performer2 or Peformer3 is female and Performer4 is male, and so forth. The objects are then placed in a three-dimensional virtual environment in the game engine along with set pieces and lighting. Each instance of the object can then be assigned a vocal track and animated to execute choreography based on their position in the line-up. I'm drastically over-simplifying here, but this is just to give us an idea.

At this point, let's assume we've faithfully recreated the staged scene. What happens from here can be dramatically different. In the stage version, the audience is sitting in seats passively watching the dancers perform. When we run the program within the game engine, we can give the audience the ability to move around the environment during the performance. We can program the Performer instances to respond to the movements of the guests and realign the choreography to always be facing the guest in the virtual environment, no matter where they navigate. Or if we want to create a Busby Berkeley-like effect, we might tell the program to multiply the Performers by hundreds and expand the choreography outward in a fractal pattern.

Despite their similarities, there are significant differences between creating with real world physics versus developing in a digital environment. Performers in real life are actual people, bound by real-world physics, energy levels, talent and physical attributes. However, the engine's Performer object can gain skills, animations, and attributes simply by referencing libraries, importing captures, and utilizing physics packages, like Neo in the film *The Matrix* who learns kung-fu in seconds by uploading the skill to his brain. The theatre audience is confined to watching prescriptive content from a distance, whereas the immersive audience enters the environment with the ability to navigate within the virtual world that is able to register their position and actions and responsively adapt the choreography.

The Narrative Paradox

Our game engine example of *A Chorus Line* is still a predetermined storyline. The experience is still limited to the functionality that has been programmed in by the developer. In their 2006 paper, "From Linear Story Generation to Branching Story Graphs," Mark Riedl and R. Michael Young noted that "even though a branching narrative may introduce variability into the experience a user has with a storytelling system, the variability is scripted into the system at design time and is thus limited by the system designer's anticipation of the user's needs or preferences."

The ability of a guest to affect the story within an experience is called agency. *When creators cling to classical storytelling methods in interactive mediums, they run into an awkward trade-off between narrative and agency; the more freedom a player has to create change, the less structure the narrative can maintain.* Consequently, the dramatic story goes flat or is eliminated completely. Conversely, if the game contains a strict linear story where a series of event must be followed through to progress a required plot, the interactions becomes stifled. This is known as the narrative paradox.

As long as we are in the mindset of *telling* stories, immersive experiences will struggle with balancing agency and narrative. Any amount of agency causes a degree of paradox.

■ ■ ■ ■ ■　　■ ■ ■ ■　　■ ■ ■　　■ ■　　　　　　■

Levels of Agency

Zero

Traditional forms of content such as film, television, theatre, visual artwork, and musical compositions are non-interactive. Audiences passively receive the story and do not interact with prearranged elements. They have Zero Agency.

Low

The most basic 360 experience contains Low Agency, or the ability to view different aspects of a story without influencing the environment or the story. Guests look around an immersive scene in whichever direction they chose and follow what interests them without regard to the creator's intent. Even with Low Agency experiences, interactivity conflicts with narrative. In Chris Milk's high-profile 360 experience *Evolution of Verse*, there's a point when a train comes barreling towards the person in the headset. The first time I viewed the experience, I was looking in a different direction and didn't see the train rushing towards me. A moment that was intended to have dramatic effect was experienced as an after-thought.

Low Agency experiences typically limit observations of non-interactive content to a specific vantage point, or move the guest along a predetermined trajectory. We call this "being on rails," like the rails of a rollercoaster that move you along the ride. Google Spotlight's stellar 360 experience *Help!*, directed by filmmaker Justin Lin, utilized "being on rails" to move the audience through an alien attack story. The experience begins with the guest soaring through city streets when an alien crash lands. As the alien descends into the subway, the guest viewpoint is automatically tracked alongside it, rushing them through subway cars and bursting back to the surface as the alien grows to an enormous size. The main female and male characters are constantly present, telegraphing where the guest should look by focusing their attention on the action, which might be through a subway window or up into the sky. This cinematically beautiful and well-composed experience was one of the most compelling 360 stories to emerge in the early resurgence of immersive technology. Part of its success was establishing a consistent movement along rails that followed a story without requiring interaction from the guest.

Local

When guests can navigate and interact with an environment without impacting the narrative of the piece, we call this Local Agency. Immersive theatre creators are championing Low Agency by allowing guests to explore scenes in a pre-scripted environment.

UK performance company Punchdrunk's immersive theatre show *Sleep No More* invites audiences to explore six floors of an abandoned hotel with more than 100 scenes happening at any given point and time. Silent audience members wearing white masks are free to follow actors behind doors to exclusive interactions or walk away from scenes at any point during the performance in search of a new storyline. Although the guests experience different sequences of events based on where they move, the overall performance remains true to the script, show after show.

Low agency video games like *What Remains of Edith Finch* likewise construct narratives as an interchangeable series of events, each pre-scripted to be navigated using different interaction techniques. Story-based video games such as *Uncharted 2* that require players to execute a series of plot points in a prescribed order to maintain the structure of the narrative also exhibit Low Agency.

Deep

Janet Murray described agency as the "satisfying power to take meaningful action and see the results of our decisions and choices." This impactful form of interaction is Deep Agency. Deep Agency allows the audience to interact with responsive characters and environments with the potential to affect the outcome of the story. Complex branching narratives are examples of Deep Agency. The narratively-driven *Walking Dead* game franchise and the episodic interactive fantasy *The Wolf Amongst Us*, both from Telltale Games, allow for Deep Agency. These episodic games allow the user to make choices that affect character development, thus emotionally connecting the player to the narrative beyond gameplay elements. In *Silent Hill 2*, the way a player choses to play and interact with the world is registered by the system to generate alternate outcomes. For example, playing your character at low health levels signifies to the game that the character is suicidal, creating a different outcome from players who maintain optimal health.

Open World

The opposite of zero-agency experiences are open-world games, such as *The Sims* or *Minecraft* where players effectively act as a God-like force on the environment. There is no authored narrative and no way to "win" the game. Players tend to project their own goals and narratives onto the world where they control the lives and environment of virtual characters at all times.

Interaction Considerations

How a guest interacts with an experience can support or interfere with their perceived agency and sensation of presence. In 2016, two VR projects at SIGGRAPH contained branching narratives, but they differed in how they exhibited agency to their guests. *Injustice*, presented by Carnegie Mellon students, allowed narrative selections through text that popped-up in-screen during the experience. Comparatively, the branching narratives of VR experience *Sequenced* were displayed in a more nuanced manner. Rather than having visible action points, *Sequenced* adapts the story based on the guests' focus. Where the guest looks determines how the story unfolds along Sam and Raven's journey, without providing feedback to the person in the experience. In this "reactive" world, the cause-and-effect of the guests' actions on the outcome of the story are completely hidden. Although interaction as an *action*, as in *Injustice*, disrupts cinematic flow, interaction as *reaction*, as in *Sequenced*, leaves the audience without the satisfaction of knowing how they are part of the story.

Baobab Studio's beautifully animated VR experience *ASTER-OIDS!* was an early attempt at balancing narrative and interactivity for general audiences. Guests in *Asteroids!* are given two hand controllers. Inside the experience, the controllers are the guests' robot arms, which can be used to interact with objects in the environment such as playing a game of catch with a robot pet named Peas. As the narrative advances, the hands become non-responsive. I watched attendees experience *ASTEROIDS!* at Sundance in 2017. Audiences loved being able to interact and play with the characters but would become uncomfortable when left standing, holding two inactive controllers/hands, during long portions of a non-interactive story.

As long as interactivity and event sequencing is limited to what the programmer coded, the narrative paradox will persist. Designers of Machine Learning systems are creating algorithms that allow computer interactions to self-evolve through the collection and statistical evaluation of data within the system. As we evolve past the need to pre-program every possible outcome, our narratives will expand beyond linear human experience.

THINKING IMMERSIVELY

Overcoming barriers to unite interactive technology and narrative has as much to do with evolving our storytelling mindset as any kind of intrinsic difficulty in coding.

In 1970, while the average American was mesmerized by the new television sets in their living rooms broadcasting Space Race updates and dialing phone numbers on a keypad instead of spinning a rotary dial for the first time, the photocopier company Xerox formed a research group in a concrete building on the outskirts of Palo Alto, California. Xerox PARC, as it was known, was a small collection of world-class researchers, scientists and engineers tasked with bringing to life a common vision: computers becoming "interactive intellectual amplifiers for everyone in the world pervasively networked worldwide."

Three thousand miles away from the starch-suited executives at Xerox's East Coast corporate headquarters, PARC's researchers rode bicycles, played table tennis and downed beers in their offbeat research facility. Dr. Alan Kay, a pioneer in computer science and one of the first people hired at Xerox PARC, later wrote, "Xerox often was shocked at the PARC process and declared it out of control, but they didn't understand that the context was so powerful and compelling and the goodwill so abundant, that the artists worked happily at their version of the vision."

The result was one of the most successful research initiatives in modern history and a number of breakthroughs that provided a foundation of information technology we still use today. Bitmap displays, overlapping windows in graphical user interfaces, desktop publishing, object-oriented programming, laser printing, and the ethernet are all credited to Xerox PARC. The PARC budget for computing in 1974 was less than 3 million dollars and yet the concepts they developed in the first five years of research and development revolutionized computing and led to a return of trillions of dollars. What was the secret to their success?

Dr. Kay attributed the success to embracing the principles of "visions rather than goals" and funding "people, not projects."

One of Dr. Kay's visions was of a "personal computer for children of all ages." He presented a paper on this concept, which he called the Dynabook, at the 1972 SIGGRAPH conference. At the time, he advised that it be "read as science fiction." In an era when computers were hefty, expensive pieces of machinery, Dr. Kay described an affordable notebook-sized computer weighing less than four pounds with the capability of bringing libraries into the home, which could also be stored locally on the device.

An early inspiration for the Dynabook was Ivan Sutherland's Sketchpad system. Developed while at MIT, Sutherland's original vision was to "make computers accessible to new classes of user (artists and draughtsmen among others), while retaining the powers of abstraction that are critical to programmers." At the time, computer interactions consisted mainly of input through command line codes, primarily to dedicated programmers. With Sketchpad, users could interact directly with objects on a screen using a light-pen.

Sutherland said he had been inspired by the 1945 essay "As We May Think," written by Vannevar Bush. Bush was an electrical engineer with a long government career that included lobbying President Roosevelt for the development of the atomic bomb during World War II. Concerned by how scientific efforts were increasingly being focused on destruction, Bush laid out his vision for a machine that could make knowledge more accessible and transferrable. Decades before the hypertexts of online content and the creation of Wikipedia, Bush described how "wholly new forms of encyclopedias will appear, ready made with a mesh of associative trails running through them." Through the shared knowledge of this Memex machine, as Bush called it, he hoped to expand our collective wisdom, lest we "perish in conflict."

Look at all this again.

Today's ubiquitous laptop was inspired by an attempt to bridge the gap between artist and machine, which in turn had been inspired by an electrical engineer's response to the atomic bomb. Each of these visionaries imagined how technology could create a better world. Understanding the limitations of their moment, they considered the potential of the tools at hand rather than the immediate capabilities.

By reconceptualizing the power and potential of story through immersive and interactive technology, my hope is that the storyplex paradigm will inspire you to redefine your current set of tools or develop new ones, invent your own processes and share them, and create something far more incredible than anyone on this planet right now could ever imagine.

In the words of Dr. Kay,

"THE ONLY WAY YOU CAN PREDICT THE FUTURE IS TO INVENT IT."

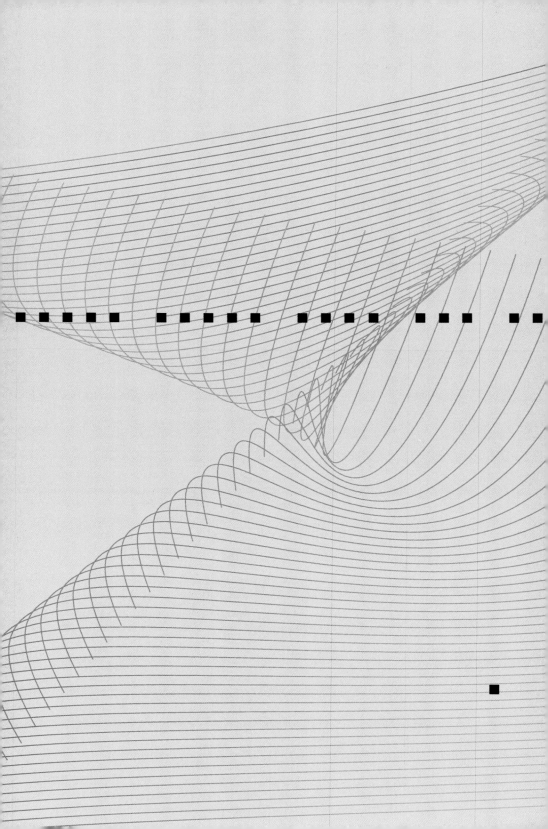

02

WHAT'S OLD IS NEW AGAIN

efore we consider the future of narratives with immersive technology, let me be clear: storytelling will not cease to exist. What it will do is what happens naturally: evolve'. How it evolves is as dependent on human nature as it is technology. We are creatures of habit. Some vestiges of storytelling will be carried forward into our immersive future, and some will remain legacies of classical mediums.

SOCIAL INTEGRATION OF MEDIA

When a new medium or technology emerges and challenges existing paradigms, it is not an easy birth. Almost every new form of media struggled on its way from an experimental concept to being fully integrated into society. Call it a fear of the unknown or technology-induced moral panic, humans have a historical pattern of resisting the unfamiliar. When train speeds began to exceed 50 miles per hour, concern grew that women's uteruses would fly out of their bodies, or that humans might just melt at such outlandish speeds. Telephones, believed to transport disembodied voices, were declared "instruments of the devil" capable of making people deaf.

As a technology evolves, techniques and equipment standardize, distribution expands, and audiences acclimate. When the fear subsides, audiences cease to gasp and be amazed. A distinct pattern of social integration emerges, with four typical stages: Demonstration, Imitation, Exploration, and Integration. Understanding how technology has been integrated in the past helps us understand our place in its current evolution.

Stage One: Demonstration

Often during the Demonstration stage, a concept exists only as a crudely functioning prototype, belying its potential. When Alexander Graham Bell attempted to sell Western Union the rights to his patented telephone, they wrote it off as being "hardly more than a toy." Early automobiles were dubbed a "horse-less carriage" fad, and the first cellphones were so costly to build that even the companies that built them thought they would never be cheap enough to replace wired communication.

Sometimes deliberately demonstrated, other times achieved by happenstance, these disruptions can seem inconsequential at the time. The first motion picture was no more than an attempt to resolve a horse-racing bet as to whether a horse lifts all four legs off the ground at once when galloping. The horses' movements were too fast for the naked eye to see, so it remained largely a friendly philosophical argument until professional photographer Eadweard Muybridge was offered 25,000 dollars to take a picture that would definitively determine whether a running horse leaves the ground entirely. Muybridge took a series of photographs of a horse running on a track. The slow shutter speed of cameras at the time resulted in blurry pictures. He reconfigured the camera's shutter mechanism and got a clearer image. In one of those pictures, all four of the horse's hooves were off the ground. Muybridge sent the photo to the press, but it was rejected for publication. It simply seemed improbable that Muybridge had achieved such a feat. So the inventor set up a follow-up experiment. This time he used 24 cameras, arranged sequentially along the track. The camera shutters were triggered by the horse's legs crossing trip wires. The rapid succession of photographs created a stop-motion effect that, when played back quickly, appeared to show a horse galloping across the frames. This time the press acknowledged Muybridge's achievement. And perhaps more importantly, live action capture was demonstrated.

Computer pioneer Ivan Sutherland, at an awards ceremony in 2014, recalled the moment that led to his creation of the first HMD in the late 1960s. At the time Bell Helicopter Company used video cameras in a remote viewing system to help pilots land at night. The system turned the viewing camera when the pilot turned his head. As Sutherland described it, "[In] one of the experiments, the observer sat in a comfortable office chair inside the building. A camera was mounted on the roof, and two people were playing catch on the roof. And the observer could watch the ball going back and forth. And then suddenly one of the players threw the ball at the camera, and the observer ducked. It was clear that the observer thought that he was at the camera and not comfortably safe inside the building. My little contribution to virtual reality was to realize that we didn't need a camera. We could substitute a computer." Inspired, he built the Sword of Damocles, the first free-standing HMD demonstrating the awe-inspiring potential of immersive environments.

The stage of Demonstration is often dominated by an introspective and isolated mindset. One or two people or groups of people out of the billions that inhabit the Earth ponder the future in scientific laboratories or tiny garages. The general public has little or no knowledge of their pursuits. But once the idea is born, it enters the cultural zeitgeist. After capturing the galloping horse, Muybridge began to develop ways to display serialized photographs in a device he called the Zoopraxiscope, a spinning disc that projected a series of images to create the illusion of movement. This device introduced movement into the static nature of the visual arts. Pictures were no longer assumed to be still images; they contained the potential to express time and motion, as Dada artist Marcel Duchamp later tried to capture in paintings such as "Nude Descending a Staircase." Thomas Edison filed patents for an invention that would record and display pictures in motion called the Kinetoscope.

Even if the conceptual demonstration doesn't ultimately work, it may spark ideas in others, who in turn can bring it to fruition through advancements in technology or revisions in process. Leonardo da Vinci never got past sketching a man flying, but that idea possessed inventors throughout the ages who sought the ability for humans to soar through the sky. One of those, Sir Hiram Maxim, used steam engine technology to build an aircraft. His prototype lifted off the ground but was uncontrollable in-flight, and he abandoned the idea. Twenty years after Maxim blew his fortune on a failed demonstration, Orville and Wilbur Wright built an airplane that could be controlled in sustained flight.

Rickety, cumbersome, and sometimes too futuristic to comprehend or outrageous to believe, these demonstrations of the future exhibit the power of raw ideas like a first breath of life: a frightening and invigorating moment when anything is possible. As a new technology enters society, changing how we live our lives and how we perceive and evaluate our existence, the artist is not beholden to the technology. In his 1965 paper "The Ultimate Display," Sutherland he saw "no reason why the objects displayed by a computer have to follow the ordinary rules of physical reality with which we are familiar." Visions during this early stage are innocent philosophical ponderings. How we ultimately reach new capabilities is a matter of tangible exploration.

Stage Two: Imitation

Once the possibilities of an idea have been practically demonstrated, early pioneers in emerging mediums tend to repurpose techniques of existing mediums. The first photographers took pictures of things in everyday life: people and landscapes. The subject matter of early films were recordings of daily life or familiar staged dramas. The first movie cameras were positioned statically, like a still camera, as people and objects moved around them. Filmmakers exploring narrative stories in their moving pictures called their creations photoplays. General audiences knew what a play was and they knew what a photograph was, so the technology was a hybrid of expectations that borrowed heavily from theatre. From the source material of scripts, to the staged acting styles and sets, the general approach to early cinema was as a recording device for theatrical performances.

During this imitation stage, the emerging technology is often rare and expensive, limiting access to a small group of experimenters. Enthusiasts with the financial means to access it tend to be well-established in a previous medium, and not surprisingly these enthusiasts repurpose techniques that have made them successful in the past. French illusionist George Méliès was a successful theatre owner and performer specializing in stage illusions and tricks. After seeing the Lumière brothers' presentation of moving images, he relentlessly sought out the rare device to install in his theatre. As he experimented with content for it, he attempted a primitive form of what we now call editing to reproduce stage effects on film. In one such experiment, Méliès began filming and detonated a magic puff of smoke in front of his actor. He then stopped the camera, had the actor leave the frame, and started cranking the camera again. The effect made the actor appear to magically vanish, an effect that he had also used during his theatrical shows. Méliès would go on to produce more than 500 films, many of which contained the same tricks that he had developed for the stage.

The first radio broadcasts functioned like audible newspapers, reporting local election results, farm reports, and weather. Early narrative television broadcasts likewise imitated the format of radio plays and the first video games imitated the real-life game of tennis, twice. *Tennis for Two* replicated two objects hitting a moving target back and forth, which would later inspire the commercial success *Pong*.

There is frequently a residual effect from the imitation of language when discussing a new technology, such as describing the measurement of automobile power as "horsepower" or calling films "motion pictures."

Imitation helps both creators and audiences conceptualize a new medium within the context of the existing world. Applying familiar techniques to a new form also makes the fundamental differences glaringly obvious. To overcome these mental limitations, creative, business, and technical pioneers have to take risks to bring a medium into its own.

Stage Three: Exploration

As social permeation of an emerging technology expands, the medium becomes more accessible to the general public and new generations of creators start to take inventive liberties, evolving forms of expression with the technology. In the Exploration phase, a new vocabulary emerges, and the technology begins to take on a life of its own, distinctly different from previous mediums.

After decades of shooting iconic pictures of New York City through the 1930s, photographer Berenice Abbott wanted to take photographs that were more than artistic; she planned to capture scientifically correct pictures of phenomenon such as kinetic energy, gravity, and electricity. "Photography can never grow up if it imitates some other medium. It has to walk alone; it has to be itself" said Abbott. When equipment she needed to shoot scientific photographs didn't exist, she invented new kinds of photographic equipment. The monopod and the autopole, a telescopic lighting rig, are now common pieces of equipment for both amateur and professional photographers.

Creators exploring new possibilities may find themselves at odds with familiar ways of doing things as they expand into new territory. Early filmmakers had hesitated to edit narrative film shots together out of fear that the disjointedness would confuse audiences. In the 1920s, as the medium's explorers began physically cutting strips of film and taping them together to condense time and space, prominent Soviet silent filmmakers contemplated whether the role of the cinema was to present a more truthful reality or to convey abstractions of reality that pointed to a higher truth. Filmmaker Dziga Vertov referred to "Cine-Eye" as the capturing of moments "inaccessible to the human eye." The quest for precision and truth that dominated Vertov's editing theory contrasted with Vsevolod Pudovkin and Sergei Eisenstein's explorations of montage as a means of influencing emotions. Pudovkin thought of each shot as raw material that would be combined for psychological effect. His explanation of editing in the book *Film Technique and Film Acting* reflects the evolution of the motion picture industry from Imitation to Exploration: "to show something as everyone sees it is to have accomplished nothing."

Stage Four: Integration

As a technology matures and complicated processes become more affordable, portable, and easily usable, they tend to become more socially acceptable. Socially, successful technologies tend to simplify to the point where they require little or no expertise to use. Professionally, the mediums themselves become more highly specialized and technical. For example, the expansion of film technologies, which evolved from silent to syncronized sound and black and white to color picture. Eventually entire industries and technologies were created to explore visual effects, sound design, and cinematography. Then when the chemical processing of film gave way to digital, digital shooting and editing became so ubiquitous and affordable that the once complex task of capturing even a single image gave way to consumer video cameras. Massive editing stations were reduced to a smartphone.

As some mediums integrate, they replace previous industries. Theatre, opera, and vaudeville venues around the country that once housed live performances were re-outfitted to showcase motion pictures. Pianos, the entertainment staple of American households in the early twentieth century, were replaced by radios, which gave way to televisions. For each generation that experiments with a technology, a subsequent generation is born with that medium already integrated into their lives. Books, once rare and confined to society's religious or intelligentsia populations, are now instantly accessible through libraries and computers. Of course there are cars, of course there are planes, of course we have lightbulbs, laptops, and late-night films. When a medium is seamlessly integrated into the fabric of society, it has reached the Integration phase.

The Integration of Immersive

Immersive technology is far from being a "new" medium. Virtual reality began as a demonstration of a conceptual idea in the 1960s, with the first wave of VR content imitating early video games. During the resurgence of VR in the 2000s, cameras with the ability to capture live action in 360 also became available, prompting filmmaking imitations. Currently, creators are exhibiting the traits of moving from imitation to the exploration phase. Retail companies have adapted AR to imitate real-world functions such as viewing virtual furniture in-home and replacing automobile service manuals. Games intended for console devices have been repurposed to VR. Films planned for traditional cameras are shot in 360. Yet, while the technology has evolved, 360 creators continue to try to "tell stories" in

"VR films," reflecting the mindset of early filmmakers making photoplays. Far from transcending the limitations of everyday physics as Sutherland envisioned, creators are imitating the reality that they know, applying familiar techniques to the new medium.

Immersive content creators often think that since their frame is now an entire sphere rather than a small rectangle, they must fill the spherical "frame" like they do in classical mediums. They place a guest in the middle of a virtual world and surround them with action in all directions without considering how to guide them through a narrative spatially. Remember, it is not just the creators transitioning into thinking immersively; our guests are, too.

I have seen thousands of people experience virtual reality for the first time. What typically happens when someone hasn't experienced an HMD before tries it, is that they enter the world and continue to look straight ahead. They assume familiar viewing habits from framed mediums until prompted to turn their heads. Their surprise at seeing the world persist in all directions is pure astonishment! Guests unfamiliar with immersive technology are accustomed to being able to see everything they need to see to understand a story in a single frame. They expect the entire frame, which they now think of as being wrapped around their head, to contain critical information. But they can only see

30 percent of the sphere at any given point in time, leading to sensations of being overwhelmed, lost, or "missing out" on the story.

When entering an experience, today's general audiences expect a story to be told, not for themselves to become participants navigating a story. But two distinct demographics seem not to suffer from this paralysis of expectation: gamers and children. Games designed to encourage interaction utilize entire virtual environments for meaningful, guided interactions, and the people who play them tend to already be familiar with navigating virtual worlds. Children also readily turn their heads inside an HMD to explore an environment, which isn't surprising considering that they haven't spent their formative years staring into framed content.

For creators and audiences trained to think that stories must be told, experiencing presence in an immersive environment often prompts questions of purpose and motivation. They ask: *What is my involvement in the interaction with the experience? Am I a passive viewer or an active participant? Should I navigate the environment, or will I be moved through it?* Guests in these early stages express the need for a clearly defined role of their place in the virtual world to alleviate confusion. As the technology becomes more developed and accessible, those needs may fade. In the meantime, creators need to be cognizant of these pre-established "framed" viewing habits and incorporate interfaces that encourage exploration.

These challenges are hallmark traits of the Imitation phase. Growing pains are inevitable as society adapts to immersive mediums, which today exist in a frustrating no-man's land: trapped by the constraints of previous mediums pushing towards the tremendous potential before us. Curiosity, experimentation, and new generations will shift us into the Exploration phase. The square mentality of classical mediums will be replaced by spherical immersive explorations. Radically different ways of approaching the medium will emerge and the new medium will come into its own.

"MEDIA, BY ALTERING THE ENVIRONMENT, EVOKE IN US UNIQUE RATIOS OF SENSE PERCEPTIONS. THE EXTENSION OF ANY ONE SENSE ALTERS THE WAY WE THINK AND ACT—THE WAY WE PERCEIVE THE WORLD. THE WAY WE PERCEIVE OUR OWN BODIES. WHEN THESE RATIOS CHANGE, MEN CHANGE."

—MARSHALL MCLUHAN—

THE HUMAN INSIDE

Regardless of how much or how fast technology advances, stories remain a human experience. But what makes a good story? Why do some bring us to tears while others are forgotten before they end? Effective story elements—ritual, components, and structure—transcend any one medium.

The Ritual of Story

When we choose to go to a live performance, we are not instantaneously teleported into the venue where the stage lights illuminate actors in mid-performance. The ritual of pre-event happenings sets expectations and prepares our imaginations to leave the real world and enter a new one.

The Gathering

An audience's experience with an event starts long before the show starts. It begins the first time they hear about it. We might learn about an art exhibit from a friend or see an online announcement for a performance. In the Elizabethan age, when many people still could not read, a flag would be raised above the playhouse to alert people that a performance would take place that afternoon: white flag for comedy, black flag for tragedy, or red flag for historical play. These first impressions signal to the audience what they can anticipate, and lead to them gathering physically or virtually at the event.

The Transition

Once the audience has gathered, ritualistic signals prepare us to absorb the story with our attention focused and our imaginations fully engaged. The stage curtains open, movie theatres dim their lights, and loading screens countdown the games' start times. The transition cues us that the experience is about to begin so we can extract ourselves from the demands of the real world to mentally and physically settle into the fictional world. We turn our phones off in the theatre or pick the game controllers up and direct our energy towards the event taking place.

Opening

The opening moments of a story set the tone. In opera, an orchestral prelude typically precedes the performance. Television shows and films play opening titles, occasionally opting for a "cold open," without a starting transition, for dramatic effect or to recount previous episodes. Everything from the font used on the title cards to the theme music signals what the audience might expect, be it heavy drama or clever comedy. Similarly, the introduction to a book is often said to be the hardest to write; all of the themes need to be introduced, and the narrator's voice and trustworthiness established.

Immersive Rituals

Carefully crafted first moments are as important for an immersive experience as for any other medium. As with traditional mediums, participants will be drawn to an experience through a gathering signal—be it an article, an advertisement, or word of mouth.

During the transition, the immersive creator merges the real world and the world of their creation. Today's awkward transitions when HMDs are involved often include crowning the guest with hardware that blindfolds them, adjusting the device for comfort, supplying outreached hands with headphones, and then placing controllers in their hands. Already a cumbersome and lengthy process compared to other mediums, few creators think beyond getting guests suited up properly unless they are presenting at a festival where they have the opportunity to build out a thematic set to convey tone and properly position the guest for the experience. At the Tribeca Film Festival in 2018, nearly all of the creators constructed miniature sets in which the hardware was placed. Guests entering the VR experience *Dinner Party*, for example, were seated around a dining room table with HMDs at respective place settings.

As the experience begins, audio-visual cues draw us into the experience similar to classical mediums. However, interactive experiences have one more critical step that must be incorporated: they must also establish the means of interacting with the world, which vary greatly and are not necessarily intuitive. Will the participants be walking through an architectural rendering, soaring through the Grand Canyon, or building a virtual avatar? Interactive conventions in an immersive environment must be established and honored, much like when children collectively agree on imaginary properties for every day objects in a sandbox. When a child comes across a stick in the sandbox, the stick can be anything that the child imagines: a wand that heals all wounds, a pet that they take care of, or a force of evil destroying invisible demons. Once the imaginative properties of the stick have been established, all the children playing with it must agree on what the stick does, else the illusion of its power disappears. If one child declares it to be a healing wand and the other says it's a pet caterpillar, then their collective imaginations will struggle to co-exist.

The "sticks" in immersive experiences are often the input controllers. The hardware is designed to be universal so that creators can assign them a wide range of functionality, from robot arms (*ASTEROIDS!*) to tree branches (*Tree*), or a paintbrush (*Tiltbrush*). Figuring out what functionality to assign to the controllers, teaching each new guest how to use it, and accommodating variations in capabilities—while making it all seem effortless and seamlessly integrated into the story—is a significant challenge. Game hardware has increasingly evolved towards more intuitive controllers. Originally navigated by assigned keyboard strokes, games can now be controlled through motion-sensing devices such as Microsoft's Kinect, which allows players to interact with games through gestures and vocal commands. Today, immersive hardware designers are exploring interactions through haptic suits with full-body motion control and sensory feedback.

Elements of Story

Immersive experiences have connected us to political struggles on the other side of the world, empowered us to overcome our anxiety, and asked us to defend against alien attackers. In every experience, a person witnesses a series of events. What exactly makes those events culminate into an effective experience? The same elements that connect us emotionally to a powerful story.

Aristotle identified what he considered to be the essentials of good drama in his seminal work, *Poetics*, after watching hundreds of performances at the Festival of Dionysus. These elements have stood the test of time, still being incorporated into modern playwriting classes and screenwriting manuals. In order of importance, Aristotle listed the elements of story as:

- plot
- character
- thought
- diction
- song
- spectacle

Both a deconstruction of drama and a reflection on human nature, these elements are foundational in immersive narratives, although it is necesssary to apply them in a different manner than one does with classical storytelling.

Plot

Aristotle considered plot, or the combination of incidents, to be the most important element of drama. Plot is traditionally a linear concept suited to premeditated writing of a script that will be performed within a frame. However, if plot is considered faithfully to Aristotle's original description, as a combination of incidents, we can trigger events in immersive mediums relative to guest interactions in the story world rather than in a predetermined sequence.

In the mid-1980s a seven-page memo circulated through Walt Disney Pictures, making its way from the mind of a freelance story analyst to the desk of then

Disney Chairman Jeffrey Katzenberg, who made it required reading for his entire development staff. Called "A Practical Guide to *The Hero with a Thousand Faces*," Christopher Vogler's memo condensed Joseph Campbell's hero's journey while adding themes from modern films as a means of creating "reliable building blocks for constructing stories, a set of tools for troubleshooting story problems." The twelve stages of the hero's journey that Volger outlined, highlighted below in capital letters, are:

> "The hero is introduced in his ORDINARY WORLD where he receives the CALL TO ADVENTURE. He is RELUCTANT at first to CROSS THE FIRST THRESHOLD where he eventually encounters TESTS, ALLIES and ENEMIES. He reaches the INNERMOST CAVE where he endures the SUPREME ORDEAL. He SEIZES THE SWORD or the treasure and is pursued on the ROAD BACK to his world. He is RESURRECTED and transformed by his experience. He RETURNS to his ordinary world with a treasure, boon, or ELIXIR to benefit his world."

Notably, Vogler thought it is not the order of the stages that is important; plot events can be shuffled around, deleted, or added to. What makes the hero's journey effective is what each "building block" represents individually: core human values and actions.

Plots in immersive experiences are more effective if they allow for, and respond to, the guests' interactions. In other words, each building block should be considered separately and individually relative to the actions of the person in the experience, rather than part of a prescribed linear narrative. This accommodates agency.

Character

Performances consist of a series of actions carried out by characters intended to elicit an emotional response from the audience. In *Poetics*, Aristotle identified character traits that created ideal characters. The first trait was moral purpose; specifically, Aristotle believed that the moral purpose of a character should be "good." This moral compass was necessary to have a character that the audience would empathize with. Second was propriety, or the character having attributes that are relevant to the story. The third and fourth traits were that the character should be both realistic, or as Aristotle said, "true to life," and consistent in their actions and words. These attributes would create characters that were credible and accessible.

Similar attributes can be found in the archetypal characters of Commedia dell'Arte, an improvisational form of theatre that was performed across Europe for over 400 years. The troupes needed easily identifiable character traits that were recognizable between towns and countries: the young lovers, the shrewd merchant, the braggadocio soldier, the gossipy old woman, the poor servant, and so on. Each character had standardized masks, costumes, and props, even identifying language and gestures. With their broad physical comedy and symbolic costumes, Commedia archetypes enacted simplistic universal plots about social climbing, thwarted lovers, and marital infidelity to the delight of audiences across a wide geographical range.

In the original *The Hero with a Thousand Faces*, Joseph Campbell identified seven character archetypes: the Hero (also the Protagonist), the Mentor (who guides the Hero), the Herald (who calls for a change), the Trickster (who provides comic relief), the Shapeshifter (who is not who they originally appear to be), the Threshold Guardian (who blocks the path of the Hero), and the Shadow (also the Antagonist). These characters represent traits rather than specific genders, ages, or philosophies. It was these traits that propelled the story's action, creating tension and relief in the plot structure.

When considered in classical storytelling, character archetypes reflect universal truths and function to drive a story's conflict and resolution. In storyplexes, they do that as well, while also providing scalable and responsive elements that can fluidly accommodate guest interactions.

Thought & Diction

Interestingly, Aristotle differentiates between what is said (diction) and what is done (thoughts exhibited through action), asserting that actions should speak for themselves without the need of a speech. A door slammed shut, for example, conveys a distinctly different context than a door being gingerly closed without making a sound. Only when a thought needs to be articulated should words be used. The element of diction referred to how the thought was expressed, or how language was used by the characters and authors.

Thought and diction are how plot and character are expressed to an audience. They are translatable across different mediums, from theatre to animation to immersive technology. The classic animation book *The Illusion of Life: Disney Animation* describes twelve principles used in Disney's animations to create expressive objects. One such principle is the "Squash and Stretch" technique, where objects are drawn with varying degrees of exaggerated physicality. A simple example of this is a bouncing rubber ball. When the ball hits the ground, the shape does not remain perfectly round; it squashes slightly as its volume encounters a solid surface. This technique of exaggerated physicality is also applied to animated characters to express feelings of resistance, fear, or love, giving animated teapots the Aristotelian equivalent of "thought."

These principles of expression can be applied to design elements beyond characters, such as interface, modes of interaction, and objects within the world, create consistency and increase believability.

Song & Spectacle

Aristotle considered song and spectacle to be non-critical elements of story. While he considered music, or song, to be the "greatest of all pleasurable accessories," spectacle was the "least artistic of all the parts." Relying on spectacle is like expecting the technology itself to be powerful enough to create a compelling experience. Truth is, the awe rarely continues past the first "wow" moments. Stunning costuming and impressive visual effects are spectacles that audiences rarely emotionally engage with, although they add to the world of the performance. Legendary filmmaker George Lucas echoed Aristotle when he said, "a special effect without a story is a pretty boring thing."

Unfortunately, immersive creators often rely heavily on the "wow" of the technology. That first moment when the guest turns around to see the world existing outside an expected frame can be spectacular. But while spectacle leaves a memorable impression, it often lacks the substance of a meaningful engagement.

Elements of Structure

Having considered the elemental building blocks of story, how those blocks come together creates the framework for an effective narrative, whether in classical or immersive mediums.

Basic Structures

On the most basic level, Aristotle concluded that a story must contain a beginning, a middle, and an end. The events shown in a dramatic performance, he wrote, must be selected and arranged for dramatic effect. Writers don't need to include every knowable detail about the lives of their characters, but rather carefully select a series of events that are unified. Each event must follow logically from one to the next, avoiding extraneous material, to attain unity. If the events in a plot occur merely post hoc, or "after" one another, that is less desirable than events in complex plots, which happen "because of" each other, or propter hoc. This distinction is even more important in interactive, immersive mediums where guests are actively navigating the narrative of the experience.

It has been said that three acts (or structural divisions) can be found in every masterpiece of story: Exposition, Conflict, Resolution. Theatre, television, radio, novels, and games have all used this structure successfully. The exposition gives the audience the background that they need to understand the circumstances of the performance and become emotionally invested in the conflict. The conflict then drives the plot forward to its resolution.

In the 1800s, German playwright Gustov Freytag noticed patterns in the structures of Greek and Shakespearean works. Typically, the action divided into five events: Exposition, Rising Action, Climax, Falling Action, and Denouement. Known as "Freytag's Pyramid," this structure continues to be a common foundation for story structure and analysis today.

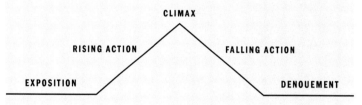

Critics of writing with an "act" structure say they yearn for more complex, less predictable stories. They are quick to point out modern exceptions to the three-act structure (*500 Days of Summer, Betrayal, Memento, Pulp Fiction*). However there are reasons for preserving it. The studies of neuroscience researcher Paul Zak specifically concluded that stories following Freytag's dramatic arc triggered the brain to release oxytocin. The fluctuation of information from rising action, climax, to falling action and denouement is suited to our attention span. Zak tracked each millisecond of the brain's activity during his studies and noted that attention "waxes and wanes" through a single 100-second video. Predictably, as the rising action occurs, the mind refocuses on the story at hand, reaching peak attention and hormonal release during the climax of the events. In other words, how the events flow from one to the next, aligning with our biological rhythms, is what's important.

Story Versus Narrative

In order to consider how we might deconstruct these elements to be useful when creating interactive experiences, it's important to first distinguish between a story and a narrative. These two words are often used interchangeably but I use them with distinct intent.

For our purposes here, "narrative" involves the human capacity for creating meaning or forming an interpretation; "story" is the events that are interpreted to create that meaning.

Let's consider stories to be the atoms of the universe. They are the building blocks in the 5 percent of matter that we can see, analyze and interact with. Narrative is the invisible "other" known as dark matter. It is the 95 percent of the universe that we can't see, nor really understand how it works, yet it exerts an undeniable force on the building blocks that we can see.

Narrative encompasses the psychology that compels us to connect with a story. It's the magic in-between the building blocks of plot and character.

Stephen King recounted how he came to write his first published novel in his memoir, *On Writing: A Memoir of the Craft*. King says two "unrelated ideas, adolescent cruelty and telekinesis, came together" when he saw an article on telekinesis being strongest in adolescent girls and then reflected back to his days as a high-school janitor, when he had to clean the girls' showers and saw tampon dispensers for the first time. He imagined these elements would make a good short story. He then describes how he expanded on the original concept by exploring his inner psyche and the relationships from his youth, modeling the main character after girls in his high school. These intangible feelings and interpreted actions were the dark matter, the memories of taunted outcasts, that provided the connective tissue which would create a powerful narrative. Eventually he expanded the short story into the full-length novel *Carrie*. The forces of empathy, pain, and acceptance brought him a 400,000 dollar pay day and launched his career as a bestselling author.

Stating "we are likely to die fighting oppression" simply does not hold the same power as the character William Wallace shouting, "They may take away our lives, but they will never take our freedom!" in the climactic scene of the film *Braveheart*. I like to think of narratives as being similar to the invisible force that holds our story galaxies together. When a writer or actor taps into the intangible force that deeply compels others, this is the dark matter of the universe in action.

Your audience will help you tap into the dark matter if you construct the story elements effectively. In the 1960s researchers at MIT's AI Lab wrote a computer program called ELIZA designed to mimic a psychological interview. The text-based program would reply to the user in the blandest possible terms, sometimes simply rephrasing their initial statement as a question. ELIZA's creator, Joseph Weizenbaum, described a typical conversation going like this:

> User: Men are all alike.
> ELIZA: *In what way?*
> User: They're always bugging us about something or other.
> ELIZA: *Can you think of a specific example?*
> User: Well, my boyfriend made me come here.
> ELIZA: *Your boyfriend made you come here?*
> User: He says I'm depressed much of the time.
> ELIZA: *I am sorry to hear you are depressed.*

Legend has it that the secretaries and staff in the lab spent hours "talking" to someone on the computer that they thought was a real therapist, revealing highly personal details to the program and even reporting that it had helped them. The project was hailed as a milestone achievement in artificial intelligence. It was one of the first programs that passed the Turing Test by exhibiting intelligent behavior indistinguishable from a human response.

Weizenbaum, however, was dismayed by the reaction. His intention had been to show that man-machine interactions were superficial, and it had backfired. In his disgust, he wrote the book *Computer Power and Human Reason: From Judgment to Calculations*, warning against research into artificial intelligence.

But ELIZA demonstrated something fascinating. Given an interaction without intrinsic meaning, people naturally projected a narrative onto the story. They "read" character into predetermined algorithmic responses. Going back to our dark matter analogy, the text inputs and outputs were like the atoms, the building blocks of the story, and the psychological interpretation was the dark matter that made it a meaningful narrative.

This principle of audience co-construction of narrative meaning is at the heart of the New York-based production company Third Rail Projects, which creates uniquely theatrical site-specific immersive experiences. Their ethereal 2017 show "Ghost Light" at Lincoln Center Theatre brought to life ghosts that haunt the fictitious Montgomery County Playhouse. When the audience entered the theatre, rather than being directed to their seats by the usher, they were lead past the rows of red chairs and behind the stage curtain. Moving in and out of dressing rooms, prop storage, hallways, and stairways through a series of overlapping choreographed dreamscapes, the audience experienced a story that folded across itself. Co-Artistic Director Zach Morris brings a similar "dark matter" narrative approach to all of their productions. Characters in Third Rail productions are not given names, only archetypes. Like ELIZA, the dialogue is specific yet vague while often acknowledging the audience's presence ("Oh, you're here," says an actor putting on make-up in the dressing room of "Ghost Light"). By doing this, Morris and his Co-Artistic Directors Tom Pearson and Jennine Willett allow space for the audience to interpret the story they're watching. The story building blocks each audience member sees may be the same, but the narratives they individually arrive at can differ dramatically.

No doubt the two words *story* and *narrative* will continue to be used interchangeably, but remember that the most complex computer programs consist of ones and zeros infinitely combined to create everything from complex backend databases to explosive three-dimensional graphics…

TO RECONCEPTUALIZE STORIES,
WE NEED TO BREAK
THEM
D
O
W
N

AND DETERMINE THE CONSISTENT
SYMBOLS THAT CAN PROVIDE
A SYSTEMATIC FOUNDATION
FOR BUILDING THE STORYPLEX
OF AN INTERACTIVE,
IMMERSIVE EXPERIENCE.

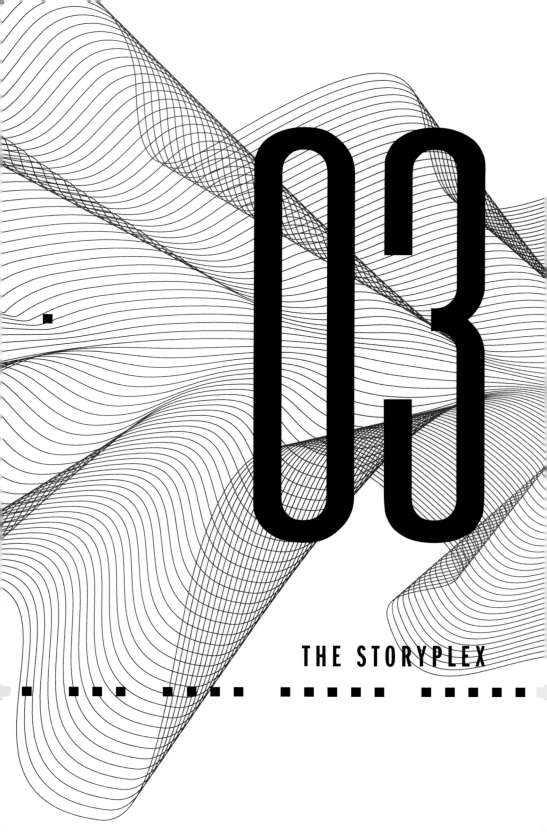

03

THE STORYPLEX

PEOPLE HAVE BEEN TRYING TO DO [VIRTUAL REALITY] STORYTELLING FOR

40 YEARS.

THEY HAVEN'T SUCCEEDED. NOW WITH OCULUS THEY'RE SAYING THERE'S A NEW STORYTELLING MEDIUM... IT'S GOOD, BUT IT'S NOT STORYTELLING. THE FACT THAT YOU'VE CHANGED THE TECHNOLOGY, AND PEOPLE ARE EXCITED ABOUT IT,

DOESN'T CHANGE

THE UNDERLYING DIFFICULTY OF
THE COMPELLING NARRATIVE

STORY.

JUST LIKE BOOKS AREN'T THE SAME
THINGS AS MOVIES. THEY DON'T HAVE
TO BE.

—ED CATMULL,
CO-FOUNDER OF PIXAR

IN *The Art of Immersion,* scholar Frank Rose observed that "every new medium has given rise to a new form of narrative." Interactive, immersive experiences will push forth narratives that contain a dynamic network of story elements, computational capabilities, and human behavior. This is the Storyplex.

The Storyplex is a dynamic network that balances the traditions of storytelling, human psychology, and the affordances of computational systems to create an immersive narrative. It is a network that can expand or contract based on the technology being used. And, within that network, the elements of story are integrated into a larger whole and influenced by a variety of environmental components, all of which contribute to a meaningful experience. The Storyplex paradigm reconsiders the constructs of narrative as well as the process of how we create immersive experiences. Done right, the technology and the storyteller disappear, and the narrative evolves as an organic extension of ourselves.

Three critical steps will help us go beyond the "tell." First, we must break free from the entrenched storytelling paradigms of classical mediums by establishing a mindset conducive to immersive thinking. Next, we should understand what tools are essential for constructing a narrative network and learn how to work with them. Finally, we will need to evolve our development process in order to address the challenges and support the capabilities of creating a Storyplex.

THE STORYPLEXING MINDSET

Language surrounding today's immersive technology is repurposed terminology from established storytelling industries that have been hacked together into a Frankenstein-esque vocabulary.

These words become mental constraints, stifling exploration and evolution. We cannot advance the art of story in immersive mediums without altering our approach to it. Nor can we create powerful experiences while chained to these conventions.

The labels "Square" and "Sphere" are admittedly an over-simplification of the contrast between how we present stories through frames, or squares, and the spherical environments that surround us through immersive technology. But they're useful. The *Square* approach tells a story within a boundary; the *Sphere* approach creates an experience within an environment.

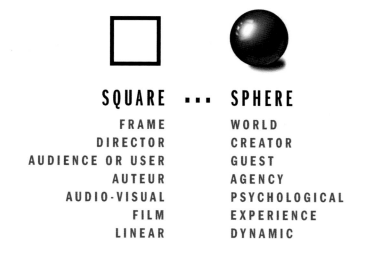

SQUARE ••• SPHERE

FRAME	WORLD
DIRECTOR	CREATOR
AUDIENCE OR USER	GUEST
AUTEUR	AGENCY
AUDIO-VISUAL	PSYCHOLOGICAL
FILM	EXPERIENCE
LINEAR	DYNAMIC

Frame vs. World

When Walt Disney needed a loan in order to build his legendary theme park, he wrote a letter to the bank trying to describe his revolutionary concept. It began: "The idea of Disneyland is a simple one: It will be a place where the hands of imagination press up against the throat of reality and squeeze without mercy." Disney continued, "When guests cross the threshold to Disneyland, they'll find themselves disoriented and nauseous as their minds and bodies adjust to stepping into a real-life dream world."

The people bringing his vision to life were the animators and designers of Disney's films. Skilled at telling stories in frames, they were now charged with designing a physical space where visitors traversed thematic landscapes at will—an island, a spaceship, a canal boat, a submarine ride, all connected by a working train. Several later admitted they had only the slightest idea what Disney was conceptualizing. After hearing him talk about his ambitious park idea, one ABC television executive flat-out said they didn't "understand what he was talking about." Disney was creating in a void with little precedence.

How he approached his vision was the key to his success. The design team built a "sandbox" where they brought in research from other attractions and amusement parks from around the world, sketched layouts for the park grounds, and posted ideas up on boards. According to Disney biographer Neal Gabler, the team underwent a "philosophical transformation" once liberated to think more broadly and immersively: "Disneyland had evolved into something much more unusual and much more grandiose—not just a park that could provide fun and diversion but a kind of full imaginative universe that could provide a unified experience."

In the spherical mentality, we demand the same evolution of ourselves as the early theme park designers: stop thinking like filmmakers, game designers, or artists building worlds containing narrative where magic can thrive.

Director vs. Creator

One of the first questions a client usually asks me is, "Are you a director?" "Director" is a familiar term to which people can nod and think to themselves, "this is the person in charge of the creative vision." In classical storytelling, the linear stories require someone to guide the path of the narrative within a framed composition. However I cringe when the word director is used to describe the lead visionary of an immersive project. They cannot control the precise sequence of audio-visual cues that a guest encounters. Some developers deflect the director title to the audience, claiming that because the audience chooses where they look, "the audience is the director!" But the audience doesn't design the stylistic look and feel of the experience, or the characters in the world, or the user interface or systems on which the experience is built. They experience a world that has been created for them. That experience was built from the vision of a creator.

By thinking of the creative visionary as a creator, we embrace the all-encompassing nature of world-building, natural fluidity of interactive experiences, and the creative freedom to redefine the rules of perception while remaining true to the narrative.

Audience or User vs. Guest

How we contextualize the person or group who interacts with immersive technology affects how we think about their involvement in the experience. I've heard these experiencers called "audiences," "users," and "players." An *audience* is a group of spectators gathered to observe an event, implying a passive interaction. The term *user* typically refers to someone who interacts with a computer or device and is too operational. *Player* suggests people taking part in a game, rather than participating in narratives. None of these terms is conceptually accurate.

I consider people engaged in immersive experiences to be participants, but the term I prefer to use when referring to participants is "guest."

Joseph Pine II and James H. Gilmore who pioneered the concept of the "experience economy" also used the term "guest" to refer to buyers of experiences. "While prior economic offerings—commodities, goods, and services—are external to the buyer, experiences are inherently personal, existing only in the mind of an individual who has been engaged on an emotional, physical, intellectual, or even spiritual level. Thus, no two people can have the same experience, because each experience derives from the interaction between the staged event (like a theatrical play) and the individual's state of mind."

People in immersive experiences have been invited into worlds of our creation, whether games, stories, or business proposals. Using the term "guest" implies a responsibility on behalf of the creators to make an experience that puts their invitees first and thoughtfully accommodates people of all backgrounds and abilities who are entering unfamiliar territory. This simple change in terminology critically aligns our thinking to the people who will ultimately experience the world.

Auteur vs. Agency

There is a particular style and rhythm to Alfred Hitchcock's thriller films. Bob Fosse's choreography is dominated by jazz hands and turned-in toes. The quirky personality of Hideo Kojima comes out in his *Metal Gear* video games. A Picasso painting is easily identifiable; it's not even difficult to recognize during which period of Picasso's life he created a particular work. Phil Spector's "Wall of Sound" formula produced a distinct layering of music that changed his industry. A fleeting moment in a Hemingway novel can run on for dozens of pages. These creators were auteurs. They originated content with boldly distinguishing characteristics without input from an audience. The audience did not choose Hitchcock's shots, influence Fosse's choreography, or contribute to Spector's Wall. Perhaps with the exception of Elizabethan groundlings throwing tomatoes at Shakespearean performers to get them off the stage, audiences in classical mediums had no input.

Does this mean that with immersive technologies, where the guest is invited to interact, there's no room for auteurs? Not entirely.

The Aristotelean elements of story are still the foundational building blocks of emotionally compelling immersive narratives. However, creators must now also consider how those elements interact with guests beyond a controlled sequence of events. No longer do creators consider only the motivations, obstacles, and rewards contained in their story, they must do the same for their guests. Having the ability to navigate and interact with the world, guests are an integral part of the storyplex and are owed the same thoughtful consideration as well-developed characters in a story. Why are they here? What is their purpose? How are their attention, decisions, and interactions influenced?

Audio-Visual vs. Psychological

Classical mediums rely heavily on audio and video technology and techniques to tell their stories. Whether we cry as we watch Rose release Jack into the ocean's abyss at the end of James Cameron's *Titanic*, laugh along with Jimmy Kimmel's late-night TV show, or catch up on world events in our Sunday morning news, classical content is a series of framed audio-visual cues. By contrast, an immersive experience is first and foremost a psychological encounter.

I was invited to film an early immersive documentary about a floating school in Makoko, Nigeria. Makoko is an ancient fishing village turned mega-slum built into the Lagos Lagoon. Almost a quarter of a million people live there without running water, electricity, or sewage. Thousands of rickety wooden shacks sit on stilts that only slightly rise above the black, polluted waters emitting a wretched stench from years of stagnant trash and debris. The "roads" of the village are darkened waterways packed with wooden fishing boats. The Makoko Floating School was a bold and innovative approach to solving several problems in the village: flooding, rapid urbanization, and education. The three-story wooden structure, designed by Nigerian-born architect Kunlé Adeyemi, floating on air-filled plastic barrels, was a communal gathering place and a school for the children of Makoko.

The producer planned to get footage by placing the 360 camera in different positions around the school. That was the primary visual: the floating school. As the creator, my challenge was to figure out how the audience would be psychologically experiencing the school. Sitting on the building wouldn't create an emotionally compelling story without zooms, pans, and cuts—the tools of a traditional documentary. I felt we would lose the details that draw an audience into a traditional story. So I had to ask myself: what is the experience of this school? What is the psychological journey that we would go on when someone inside the headset came to Makoko?

As we traveled to the school by boat, journeying away from land in a maze-like series of twists and turns, the waterways got wider and wider. When we reached the outskirts of the crowded huts on stilts, the bright blue roof of the floating school rose iconically above the rusted tin rooftops of the village. That, I realized, was why we were there. The most powerful experience was the journey to the school with the school children. In the experience, guests would travel on a boat with these children, through their maze of impoverished struggles, and just as the journey seemed endless, the floating school would rise out in the distance like a beacon of hope, as it did for Makoko's children. There was a significant problem with this shot, however. We needed to stabilize the camera on a wooden boat filled with children without having a crew member in the shot, which might pull the guest out of the immersion. We were shooting with a PTGrey Ladybug that had to be hardwired to a laptop for power and storage. This early camera footage contained a nadir, a black area on the bottom of the 360 shot, which I reasoned was where I could hide—if we could get the camera stabilized on my head. The technical director gaff-taped the camera mount to a bicycle helmet for me to wear while sitting on the boat with the children. It was a big risk, especially considering the potentially nausea-inducing low frame rate of the capture. So, I decided I would also get a "safety" shot—one that I knew could be executed without technical complications. The safety would be the original concept: a static shot on the floating school. It was a visually-based shot; one that I rolled off as backup without much thought towards the audience experience.

Back in the editing room in New York, I looked at both takes in a headset. The journey on the boat was incredible. I was part of an environment that was naturally evolving and taking me with it. Meanwhile, the shot on the school itself was relatively uninspiring. There was no context for the psychology of that particular viewpoint. I didn't know why I was there or why I should care about what I was seeing. Starting with an audio-visual driven "camera shot" resulted in footage that was not nearly as compelling as when I took the time to consider the psychological experience of the guest.

Film vs. Experience

I was usually met with blank stares when explaining virtual reality to family and friends in the late 1990s, telling them they could be Godzilla and destroy Pittsburgh by blowing fire out of their mouth. It was a stretch for their imaginations that they could fully embody a character in a virtual world. In the basement of the massive concrete bunker called Wean Hall on Carnegie Mellon's campus, we were building bizarre alternate realities experienced through a device strapped to your face running off a Pentium 3000 running Windows 98. Everything was built with computer graphics and was interactive. Twenty years later, more advanced cameras and sophisticated non-linear editing systems added 360 live action capabilities to the industry. Inevitably filmmakers began to experiment with telling stories in 360 videos. Prominent film festivals such as Sundance, Cannes, Venice, and Tribeca began exhibiting immersive content, conveniently calling the new medium "VR films."

The re-appropriation of common terminology makes the unfamiliar accessible, but it also limits the audiences' expectations and confines the imaginations of creators. In immersive experiences, we want our guests to explore their environments and feel as though they were in another world, not passively stare at a rectangular screen. By referring to these creations as "experiences" rather than "films," "movies," or "videos," we can let ourselves and our guests embrace the medium's unique opportunities.

Linear vs. Dynamic

When Romeo discovers Juliet's lifeless body in Shakespeare's famous story of star-crossed lovers, he, stricken with grief, drinks the apothecary's poison. There is no alternative course of action; nothing else to watch on stage; no parallel universe exists where Romeo waits for his love to awaken. The play takes place before us with a predetermined plotline of events that escalate into a heartbreaking climax as the audience watches, unable to affect the story.

By contrast, plots, characters, actions, environments, and interfaces in interactive mediums can be dynamically generated. Computers respond to players actions as they build underground fortresses with a group of dwarves in *Dwarf Fortress*, solve puzzles to rescue a princess in *Legend of Zelda*, and drive through cities in the hijacked cars of *Grand Theft Auto*. In interactive virtual worlds, guests similarly navigate through environments interacting with objects, characters, and stories. The *Fantastic Beasts and Where to Find Them VR Experience* teaches guests how to cast spells while in *Gnomes & Goblins*, guests toss walnuts and explore a gnome's treehouse. The computer system procedurally generates the world.

As machine learning and artificial intelligence advance and are increasingly applied to narrative, we will be able to move beyond gameplay to create emotionally-driven dynamic and responsive stories not possible in classical storytelling.

THE STORYPLEXING TOOLBOX

THERE'S A SAYING: *If all you have is a hammer, everything looks like a nail.* Philosopher Abraham Kaplan called it the "Law of the Instrument," and psychologist Silvan Thompkins described it as the "tendency of jobs to be adapted to tools, rather than adapting tools to jobs" in his "Computer Simulation of Personality" essays. When we rely on limited tools, or the wrong ones, we mentally bias our solutions and impede our progress. Before we start building immersive experiences, let's make sure we are working with a full set of tools. The storyplexing toolbox here is structured based on observations from hundreds of projects. I integrate the sections and components fluidly into my process—sometimes relying more heavily on certain tools, other times not using ones at all. Most importantly, this range of tools allows my teams and me to work effectively with an immersive mentality. I have found that if the entire development team—the executives, creatives, engineers, and designers—refers back to these tools, it helps the team maintain immersive thinking, and the resulting product is greatly improved.

The storyplexing toolbox has three sections:

TECHNOLOGY
CREATORS
PARTICIPANTS

Each of these sections is of equally critical importance. *Technology* consists of the practical hardware and software used to create virtual environments. *Creators* are the individuals involved in the production of experiences. *Participants* are the guests who experience immersive projects.

As we open our storyplexing toolbox, remember that our imaginations, more than any technology, are the driving force behind the illusion of immersion.

THE STORYPLEXING TOOLBOX:

COMPUTER ENGINEERING has an unfortunate reputation for existing at the opposite end of the creative spectrum from narrative. Stories are expected to connect us to the intangible and ethereal, to unpredictable expressions of the human soul. Computer science, on the other hand, is widely assumed to deal with exact functions and practical applications, the act of creating something with an intentional outcome. I have known many classical artists to be deterred by the mere thought of writing lines of programming code. And yet computers, software, and hardware are fundamental tools of this new medium, whether you're using immersive technology to augment live interactions or as the primary means of experiencing content..

The computational components you choose to work with will have a significant impact on what you build, how you can release it, and the look and feel of the final product. New technologies are being developed and released on a weekly, if not daily, basis. They typically fall into one of four categories, based on the senses that they affect or the role they play in development:

- Visual Display Systems
- Content Capture Systems
- Audio Systems
- Haptic Systems

TECHNOLOGY

VISUAL DISPLAYS SYSTEMS

Blurring the line between real and digital involves merging physical visual cues with digital ones. As seen in our Immersive Cheat Sheet, visual display systems can overlay, insert, or completely replace what we see in the real world. Three types of visual displays currently dominate immersive technology: Head-Mounted Displays, Mobile Devices, and the Magic Window.

Head-Mounted displays, or HMDs: These socially awkward devices currently look like bricks strapped to people's faces. Today, HMDs remain connected, or *tethered*, to a high-powered computer through cables for maximum processing power, supporting higher quality graphics and increased interactivity. But once you've seen people wearing HMDs unknowingly wrap themselves in the cables or yank the cables out of the computer port, you know why wireless functionality is a primary focus for the next generation of high-powered HMDs.

Mobile Devices: To increase mobility and portability, Mobile VR devices use smartphones' internal computing capabilities, high-resolution screens, media storage, and pass-through cameras as the hardware for virtual and augmented reality systems. These pocket-sized devices are more powerful than the computer systems that sent a spaceship to the moon—and they are everywhere. Google leveraged the ubiquitous mobile phone technology to bring 360 content marketed as "virtual reality" to the masses by shipping over a million Google Cardboards to *New*

York Times subscribers. The Cardboard device was a folded-up piece of—you guessed it—cardboard with a set of plastic lenses. Recipients had to download the *New York Times* VR application on to their phone, and the app launched with the journalistic 360 experience, "The Displaced." Subscribers inserted their phone into the cardboard device and held the device up to their eyes to look around the environment of children forced from their homes during the global refugee crisis. In Mobile VR, the smartphones are the viewing mechanism, display device, and processing unit.

Magic Window: Guests can also experience immersive environments by looking into them through a framed device. Smartphones and computer screens create a "magic window" which can be rotated or screen-swiped to change the direction the viewer faces. Technical purists don't consider 360 video to be true VR because it is contained within a rectangular screen, and generally the content has little or no interactivity. However, 360 videos psychologically evolve the framed mindset by letting viewers navigate an environment inside the magic window. Suddenly, the frame does not contain the whole experience, but is merely a window into another world. Gamers have been doing this for decades, but as more mainstream consumers adapt to immersive technology, 360 video is a necessary stepping stone in the cultural integration of VR. The inexpensive production pipeline and broad audience reach on social media platforms such as YouTube360 and Facebook360 allows businesses to experiment with the medium with minimal investment, and allows audiences to adapt to the capabilities of immersive environments in small increments.

Many augmented reality applications use the pass-through camera on smartphone devices to create a "magic window" through to the real world. Digital content is then overlaid on top of the image of the real world. This was the set-up for the gaming phenomenon *Pokemon Go,* which brought AR into the mainstream in 2016. Using the mobile device's GPS to determine a player's position, Pokemon characters would virtually appear. Players could then "catch" them by throwing virtual pokeballs at them.

■ ■ ■

Pros and Cons of Visual Displays Systems: Hardware and software races will continue for the foreseeable future, following the typical technical development pattern of humanity perpetually trying to find a faster, cheaper more powerful solution. What's important here is not the functionality of each piece of equipment, but awareness of their capabilities.

In today's hardware, there is essentially a trade-off between accessibility and power. 360 videos are easily accessible by computer and smartphone, but are lower quality with little or no immersive value. Mobile VR at least creates a sense of immersion and is portable, but there are significant constraints on performance. Powered HMDs add layers of computational power, more advanced head-tracking, room-scale positional tracking, dedicated motion control, multi-user functionality and more. It is also a more expensive option, requiring a dedicated minimum-viable computer and consequently has far less market permeation.

CONTENT CAPTURE SYSTEMS

Content displayed in virtual environments is created through content capture systems. Many of the current tools have been adapted from filmmaking and gaming industries. Like the Visual Display Systems, there will be trade-offs depending on which systems you use.

Cameras: A wide variety of 360-degree camera rigs can capture the entire sphere of a realistic environment with varying degrees of quality. Similar to a traditional camera, the content captured by these rigs is a two-dimensional image. Each camera records the footage from the direction it is facing. Those angles are then "stitched" together to create a spherical image. When you look at the stitched 360 footage inside a headset, you'll notice that you cannot move left or right, up or down; like traditional cinematography, the only point of view you have with this type of capture is from that exact position of the camera.

Consequently, navigation within a 360-camera captured environment beyond the pre-recorded position of the camera is significantly limited.

Game Engines: To create a virtual environment that guests can navigate through, worlds are built in game engines. Game engines are software packages that support core interactive functions in three-dimensional world-building. The developers of engines such as Unity and Unreal have done the heavy-lifting of building a world from scratch by providing the underlying code to control everything from 3D objects, the physics of the world, and the user interface in a single platform. There's a reason they are called "game" engines—this software is built for interactivity. The price of that functionality is realism.

Digital Content: Content for virtual environments can also be imported from other software programs including:

- Images and videos from traditional digital sources
- 2D and 3D computer-generated or animated content
- Computer-Aided Design (CAD) drawings such as architectural and design models

Volumetric Capture Systems: Still in an early stage of development, volumetric capture systems show significant promise in helping creators find a balance between realistic capture and interactivity. These processes create three-dimensional representations of real world objects through different types of

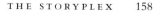

depth-mapping techniques: light field capture, volumetric capture, and photogrammetry.

The concept of light fields, namely that our world is filled with bouncing rays of light, has been around since the mid-1800s. Capturing light fields is a complex problem involving recording the direction, color and intensity of light rays from different angles. Camera companies have developed devices that capture fields of light rather than a single light image. This information is then used to alter the image after it has already been taken to create what has been described as "living pictures with variable depth of field."

Volumetric Capture uses an array of cameras to record a physical object from multiple angles simultaneously. The data is then combined to create a 3D model of the object. When I was working with Dr. Takeo Kanade, computer vision professor in the Robotics Institute at Carnegie Mellon, he was building a predecessor for volumetric capture which contained 51 cameras mounted in a geodesic dome. The original concept was expanded by CBS to create Eye Vision, which was used for the 2001 Super Bowl. During the broadcast, 21 synchronized cameras covered 210 degrees of the Tampa Bay stadium, allowing for playbacks that could fly around the field, showing multiple angles. Today companies like 8i and Scatter are recording smaller areas, such as a single human figure, through a similar process. This allows them to create actual 3D objects, with greater detail.

TECHNOLOGY

Photogrammetry takes the concepts of multiple camera angles and applies it to larger static objects or locations. By taking pictures from hundreds of different angles at different times, they create a database of information from which an interactive 3D model can be constructed. Because the model is built and textured from the real-world photos, this painstaking process is useful for creating a photo-realistic duplication of an environment.

Volumetric capture systems face considerable technical and artistic hurdles before they can reach an acceptable level of realism for general audiences. Implementation is costly and access is limited, making cameras and game engines, or a combination of the two, the dominant content capture systems for most developers today. The content capture system influences the look and feel of an experience.

CASE STUDY:

Every afternoon in middle school, my childhood dog, Maggie, would come trotting up the hill to meet me at the bus stop. The sun would shine high above the tall pine trees that lined an unevenly paved road leading down to our little white house near the river. Let's create a virtual simulation of an afternoon on the street I grew up on in Marietta, Gerogia to explore the differences between types of content capture systems.

If realism is important to our experience, we could capture the street with a live-action 360 camera rig. Because the cameras are capturing a spherical image, we are not able to reframe for different close-ups. The audience would only be able to move through the street exactly as the camera captured it. If they are deathly afraid of dogs and Maggie comes running up to them, they have no choice but to continue along the filmed path.

If we wanted to give the guest the ability to move away from Maggie, we need to build-in interactivity. We could build the street in a game engine. To do so, we need to create all the elements of the street digitally: the sun shining, the trees swaying, the grass along the edges of the pavement, and of course, a digital Maggie. All the elements of the scene, the rules of the world, and the interactions are coded into the world.

Digital scenes constructed for film scenes are "pre-rendered," meaning that a computer processes, or "renders," the calculations of the scene and exports a linear clip, which can then be imported into a film or video game like a traditionally filmed sequence. To give you a sense of how complex those scenes can be, it took an average of 29 hours to render a single frame for Pixar's animated film *Monsters University*. A scene in virtual reality has to be rendered by the engine in real-time, ideally 90 times every second. In order to do that, the scene has to be significantly less detailed than a Pixar film.

To understand how much less, let's take one element from our scene in Marietta: the sun. If the sun is created as a square, it would consist of six sides that would have to be rendered 90 times each second relative to where the guest moves. If we wanted the sun to have a curved surface to be a more realistic sphere, we would need to increase the number of "sides," or polygons, so as to appear smooth. Let's say we need 300 polygons to create a believably curved surface. Now that the computer must calculate the positions of each of those 300 polygons relative to the user's movements 90 times every second, the load on the engine has significantly increased. And with the more details you add to the street—lamps, buildings, trees—you add to your polygon count. The more polygons, the more load on the system and the more likely you are to endure dropped frames and reduced frame rate, which can create nausea. To optimize and streamline real-time rendering, game engine projects tend to be stylized rather than realistic.

6 POLYGONS · · · · · · · · · 300 POLYGONS

To overcome rendering limitations, we could incorporate live-action footage in the 3D environment. For example, we could film the street with multiple 360 camera positions to capture the photo-realistic environment at different angles. Inside a game engine, each position might have "hotspots," or points of interaction, where guests transition between 360 camera locations or activate other digital components.

AUDIO SYSTEMS

Surround sound in cinemas and theatres are typically transmitted to an audience through stationary speakers attached to the venue walls. In immersive experiences, spatialized sound localizes the sound based on an object's or a guest's movement in a virtual environment. If you move closer to a bumblebee in the virtual environment, then its buzzing hum will sound closer to you. Creating three-dimensional, navigable soundscapes is the realm of immersive audio.

There are two parts to creating spatialized sound: capture and design. Like traditional filmmaking, capture is done through recordings devices. Spherical ambisonic devices contain multiple microphones pointed in different directions, allowing it to record sound along the traditional x axis as well as covering sounds above and below the device. Recordings are then processed through software that designs the placement and playback of the sounds. Effective use of spatialized sound allows creators to direct attention and motivate interactions in virtual environments.

CASE STUDY:

In 2017, Scilla Andreen, CEO and Co-Founder of IndieF-lix which distributes independent films, approached me about creating a VR experience to help guests understand first-hand what happened when young adults had a panic attack. Her goal was to create an experience that was both a means for creating empathy and a tool to help children who suffer from panic attacks. The first-person perspective and need for a realistic setting worked well with a 360 camera content capture system. It was important to IndieFlix that the project reach as many people as possible, so distribution would need to be through a downloadable app to MobileVR. By creating an interactive sound design inside Unity, we could build an experience that was different for each guest. I collaborated with Hollywood sound designer Scott A. Jennings and Jeffery Phaklides to create an interactive soundscape. First, we captured all of the sound on location in the live experience with an ambisonic microphone. Select set pieces and props were placed as "triggers" that would increase the level of anxiety each time a guest focused on them in the virtual experience. When actor Em Grosland performed the narration, they recorded both the scripted lines and improvised multiple levels of anxiety for each trigger. The 360 video was then imported into Unity, where invisible objects were placed in the environment, matching objects in the visual room. We then designed a grid system by which the triggers would escalate and respond when "triggered" by the viewer's gaze. The result was a highly personalized experience that was profoundly effective at creating a responsive environment, even within a 360 video.

HAPTIC TECHNOLOGY

Haptic technology physically connects guests to virtual worlds through the sensation of touch. Video game companies implement haptic technology in their controller devices such as the vibrating Nintendo Rumble Pak and steering wheel controllers that give the sensation of resistance when turning in a racing game. In the mid-90s, every virtual world we created had custom-built "haptics." For the *Spider-Man* world, the player was given haptic gloves with sensors on the middle finger and palms. By pressing your fingers to your palm à la Spider Man, virtual streams of webbing shot out. The player was able to "swing" around Gotham by slinging webs to nearby buildings where the web would attach to the surface and pull you over to it. Transitioning from left-palm to right-palm sent you web-sling-flying through the city. Other haptics let the player lean left and right in a mining cart to select a track to zoom down as Indiana Jones, flap their arms to fly across a planet, or pour glass after glass of wine to see how virtually inebriated they would become. Such is the imagination of college students. We were fearless in our pursuit of haptic controls. They created a cognitive bridge between the virtual environment and physical presence.

As immersive technologies entered the consumer market in the 2010s, mass-producible controllers replaced highly specific haptic devices. Like generic gaming controllers, these devices have triggers, buttons, and pads that can be assigned functionality. The trigger button on a Vive controller can make balloons, shoot arrows, or become robot arms. In Sony's 2017 *Spider-Man: Homecoming* VR experience, the trigger button on the controllers activated Spidey's webstrings.

Start-up research companies as well as research departments in mega-media corporations are developing complete haptic systems. These range from mechanized gloves to suits covering the entire body. The promise of being able to tangibly feel the virtual world as if we were in *Ready Player One* are more than academic, they are necessary to complete the sensation of immersion.

THE STORYPLEXING TOOLBOX:

PRESENCE MULTIPLIERS

Certain effects can exponentially help increase a guest's sensation of presence in a virtual environment or severely detract from an otherwise enjoyable experience. We call these *multipliers*. Visual multipliers include proper tracking and low-latency, which allow the visual virtual world to remain consistent with the guest's physical movements. Spatialized sound is an audio multiplier. Haptic multipliers include intuitive interaction controls. Location-based VR experience developers such as The Void create haptic presence by placing guests within a physical environment wearing HMDs so that object encountered in the virtual world directly correspond to objects in the physical environment. For example, when you walk across a virtual bridge in the *Ghostbusters Dimension* experience in New York City, your hand can reach out and hold on to a real-world bridge. Several studies have shown how sensory feedback that properly aligns with our mental models of a virtual environment enhances the sensation of presence. Conversely, negative multipliers can leave guests confused or frustrated. These include complicated modes of navigation, non-intuitive interaction methods, and lag time between real world actions and the corresponding updates in the virtual world.

CASE STUDY:

I worked with Ken Perlin's Future Realities Lab at NYU to create *Holojam in Wonderland*, in which co-located audience members and multiple actors experienced the same virtual story in mobile VR headsets. The audience puts on their headsets in the real-life location designed to look like a Victorian parlor. Inside the headset, real-life objects such as a birdcage are replicated in the virtual world, and now with a virtual bird inside. During the experience, Alice, played by a live actor also in a headset, magically transforms her rainy day Victorian parlor into a luscious Wonderland, talking and moving around the virtual and real world simultaneously with mobile audience members before encountering a rushing, talking Rabbit, also played by a real actor tracked in the physical space. At a key point in the narrative, the characters and guests "shrink" in the virtual world as the environment scales to enormous proportions. To maintain the illusion of scale, the actors voice was then delivered from an overhead speaker in the ceiling. While speaker placement is a practical solution, more complex spatialized sound systems are developing.

THE STORYPLEXING TOOLBOX:

ADAPT THE TECH OR ADAPT TO THE TECH

If you run into a problem where the technology doesn't support your vision of an experience, you have two options. You can adapt the technology to suit your needs, or you can adapt your vision to suit the technology. For example, if you want to create an experience where multiple players in a game are networked in real-time, you can use the networking capabilities available in the existing gaming engine. If those systems won't allow you to easily add players, support a high volume of players, or otherwise support functionality you want, you will either have to reduce your vision of how the experience will be played or build your own scalable network and interface from scratch. A skillful team with the same traits will adapt the technology to reach the goal envisioned.

TECHNOLOGY

THE GROUP OF PEOPLE conceptualizing and implementing the technology to create a storyplex are the Creators. Designers, engineers, creators, and visionaries all contribute to the success of an interactive experience. Ideally, the immersive team is well-balanced and interdisciplinary, and speaks multiple "languages" of narrative, engineering, and design.

CREATORS

In classical terms, the lead creator would be called the director. Leading the artistic, dramatic, and interactive vision for an experience, the creator helms the designers and engineers and guides decision-making for the project. They translate between the language of computers, narrative, and most importantly, the guests. Creators who act as if they are dictators, who are unwilling to listen to the suggestions and concerns of their designers, engineers, and other team members, run the risk of alienating their audience in the name of auteur control and missing creative solutions.

VISIONARIES

Visionaries lead the development of an experience, often making creative, financial, and distribution decisions for the project. There are several visionaries on an immersive project.

Business Visionaries: It took years for Chester Carlton, inventor of the Xerox electrophotographic process, to convince

CREATORS

manufacturers to build a machine using his revolutionary concepts. Even then, it took decades of persistence for them to engineer a working model of an electrophotographic copier machine. When Morton Heilig pitched his concept of the "Sensorama" as an immersive showroom display device to corporations such as Ford and International Harvester, no one invested. He built and installed a single unit at Universal Studios, only to have it pulled for not being family-friendly. He and his wife took on enormous debt to build their vision of the future of entertainment, an investment that she claims to still be paying off today. Walt Disney had a vision of creating a feature-length animated film. As the 250,000 dollar budget for *Snow White and the Seven Dwarfs* climbed past an unprecedented 1.7 million dollars, he and his brother, Roy, approached the Bank of America for a loan. The bank vice president, Joe Rosenberg, had already asked around the industry about the project and been told not to put a dime into "Disney's Folly." After watching an incomplete rough cut with the missing parts acted out by Walt, Rosenberg took the leap of faith that completed the film that created an empire. Business visionaries are critical. These are the people willing to take risks to back the next Heilig and fund the next Disney.

Producers: "Producers are the ones who get movies made," wrote legendary film producer Christine Vachon in *A Killer Life*, "from the concept to the contracts to bankrolling the folks at the craft services table." The same is true in immersive experiences:

producers have a hand in making just about everything happen from forming teams, finding financing, managing development, to wrangling distribution. Producers are the grease that gets the wheels to turn.

DESIGNERS

As in classical mediums, a variety of skilled designers guide the audio-visual elements of a production.

Narrative Designers: Narrative designers craft the use of story elements within an experience. Writing is only part of what they do, taking into consideration the emotional arc of the experience as presented by characters. They also consider the actions of guests present in the environment, who can sometimes affect change within the story. They understand the limitations and advantages of immersive technology and work closely with experience designers and engineers to create a seamless narrative.

Experience Designers: Experience designers contribute to the layout and delivery of information to the guest through graphical interfaces and interaction design, including interactions between the system and the end user. These designers also conduct user-testing to determine where the guest interactions play out as expected, or where the experience loses its intuitiveness and becomes confusing.

Content Designers: The visuals of the world are created by the content designers. These can be the members of the camera

CREATORS

crew filming the live action 360, animators, and visual effects developers. Graphic designers model virtual objects and characters, texture those models with patterns, and animate the actions of the objects in an environment. Each of these designers has a sensibility for their highly specialized craft.

Audio Designers: The audio designer envisions the soundscape of the experience through a mix of live action recordings, sound effects, and musical soundtracks. They design the on-set capture system, which is supplemented by libraries of material during the post-production process.

ENGINEERS

Coding Engineers: These folks speak the language of programming. Engineers are the gateway power of interactive, immersive technology. Their expertise can range from backend engineers (server, database, and server-side applications), frontend developers who work with client-facing elements, and delivery engineers who are familiar with porting experiences to various hardware devices.

Sound Engineers: When the live sound is captured on location, it is brought into the sound engineer's studio. Here the aural composition of the experience comes alive through technical mixing of music, sound, and effects. In immersive environments, the output of an audio engineer can range based on the technology available.

- Stereo: Audio to both ears, regardless of head position
- Binaural: Replicates sound in two separate ears, fading between directions based on head rotation around one axis.
- Ambisonics: 3D sound field that supports head rotation in every direction

STANDING ON THE SHOULDERS OF GIANTS

Decades of research into virtual reality, presence, haptics, augmented reality, perception, interactive narrative and more are at your fingertips. Academic research, industry organizations, presentations and studies are all resources for information. From the autonomous agents work of Joseph Bates; the interactive fiction projects from Michael Mateas; early research into the future of narrative by Janet Murray; mind-bending insights from the man who popularized the term "virtual reality," Jaron Lanier; to Scott Fisher, Brenda Laurel, Skip Rizzo, and Nonny de la Pena, many intelligent and creative developers have been exploring immersive experiences for decades. Even outside the realm of immersive technology, researchers in neuroscience, artificial intelligence, human-computer interaction, and developers in immersive theatre, game design, and engineering have grappled with the complexities of experiencing immersive, interactive worlds. These brilliant minds left behind breadcrumbs, not knowing where they might lead. It is up to today's creators to follow them, contribute to their path, and see where it takes us.

CREATORS

THE STORYPLEXING TOOLBOX:

THE THIRD ASPECT of the storyplexing toolbox is one you won't find in classical mediums. Yet it is equally important as both the technology and the creators. Immersive experiences cannot happen without Participants. In a storyplex, participant interactions are proactively considered and incorporated into the design. Guests trust us to partially or completely obscure their field of view, to change their hands into robot arms or dragon wings, and to lead them safely through an interactive landscape. We must not fail them. Let us empower our guests beyond their wildest dreams — to share experiences that profoundly affect their lives, expand what they imagine to be physically possible, and open their consciousness to other dimensions of communication and understanding. We start by considering them as part of our development process.

When theme park designers from Disney ranks describe their process, they always begin with and return to the guest experience. From Anaheim to Shanghai, everything designed, built, rehearsed, and performed is part of the business of creating happiness for guests. To sustain an atmosphere of trust and enjoyment for every one of the thousands of visitors a day that came to the park, Walt Disney outlined Four Keys. These principles defined standards for guest interactions at Disneyland, in order of priority:

- *Safety:* Safety should never be sacrificed to achieve any other goal. Whether it's a theme park or a virtual world, the guests need a safe environment—from clearly understandable instructions to employees practicing safe behaviors. And when enforcing safety resulted in a negative experience for a guest, Disney looked for ways to improve the situation. For example, if ride administrators had to turn children away for being too short for a ride after waiting in a long line, they gave the child a pass to skip the line on their next ride.

I have seen people go to the hospital because of safety constraints being bypassed in the name of rapid development, for example by removing the safety borders in a Vive experience and not having spotters for guests who are entering virtual reality for the first time. In order for our guests to fully embrace an experience, they must feel safe to explore an unfamiliar space without being hurt.

- *Courtesy:* More than simply being nice, Disney intended "courtesy" to mean going the extra mile for guests. Cast members were expected to find ways to make the guests' experience more enjoyable. An example used in Disney training was answering a guest's question, "What time is the 3 o'clock parade?" Rather than responding with the head-scratchingly obvious, the cast member would ask more questions to understand what the guest was really asking. Are they wanting to know at what time the parade will get to their spot in the park, which may be up to half an hour after the start time? The concept of Courtesy extends to an effort to accommodate every guest, including both children and parents, non-English speakers, and guests with disabilities. What is the implication for creators here? Rather than considering first what story you want to tell, or your easiest means of navigation through an experience, see the world through the eyes of the participant first. At festivals and conferences around the world, I've seen docents shout navigation instructions at guests in headsets, describing what button to press to make something happen in the world. The guest fumbles with the controllers while a voice yells "Press the 'up' button!" or "Grab the blue box on your right!" Ideally, this should never happen. Extend the courtesy of designing an experience that accommodates guests of all abilities, as much as possible.

- *Show:* In the book *Designing Disney: Imagineering and the Art of the Show*, legendary animator and show builder John Hench describes having every element of a theme park contribute to guests' experiences. "Designing the guest's experience is what Walt [Disney]'s Imagineers came to call 'the Art of the Show,' a term that applies to what we do at every level, from the broadest conceptual outlines to the smallest details, encompassing visual storytelling, characters and the use of color." Disney's element of Show included cast members always staying in character while in view of the guest. Similar consistency in design, presentation, and atmosphere sustains the illusion of magic for the guest and should be a goal in any immersive experience.

- *Efficiency:* Disney parks are expected to be managed efficiently, and that included the cast members managing their time and resources well. It also means letting the employees directly solve guest problems rather than going through a slew of bureaucracy. Efficiency in design helps guests have an optimal experience, and efficiency in coding allows systems to run optimally.

HUMAN-COMPUTER INTERACTIONS

Skillful immersive design includes adapting cognitive psychology principles to overcome usability challenges, which has been widely studied in the interdisciplinary field of Human-Computer Interaction. HCI focuses on the usability of a system by uniting research from psychology, design, and computer science to inform development decisions that reduce user errors and make systems intuitive to use. One of the most renowned resources on the psychology of design is Donald A. Norman's book *The Design of Everyday Things*, which identifies key principles that impact usability and can help us create optimal and enjoyable immersive experiences, including Visibility, Cognitive Load, Constraint, and Consistency.

PRINCIPLES FOR CREATING IMMERSIVE EXPERIENCES

The Visibility Principle

The visibility principle states that the more visible functions are, the more likely users will be able to know what to do next. For example, when the numbers on telephones had numbers as well as multiple letters (1-ABC, 2-DEF, etc.). To dial a phone number was visually simple—press the number. However, as those of us with early flip phones will remember, writing a text involved pressing a button multiple times in order to scroll through upper and lowercase letters that corresponded with numbers on the di-al-pad. The process of revealing the hidden letters was time-consuming, error-prone, and frustrating. The reverse application of the visibility principle is important to remember with immersive technology: when something is not in view, it is difficult to discover or interact with.

Cognitive Load

In cognitive psychology, cognitive load refers to the total amount of mental effort being used in the working memory. Computer interface designers minimize the "noise" in interfaces by removing unnecessary visual elements. Elements with an immediately recognizable purpose or trait such as a trash icon or character archetype helps to reduce cognitive load.

Constraint

Another way to reduce cognitive load is through the principle of constraint. Constraint is a restriction on the kind of interaction that can take place at a given moment. If one big red button is on a console, there is only one button the player is likely to push. If the console has hundreds of buttons, switches, levers, and slides, then the brain must work through what each button is, what it will do, and if it should be selected—increasing the mental effort required.

Consistency

Reducing cognitive load can also be accomplished through consistency in design. This principle states that design interfaces and experiences should have similar operations and use similar elements to achieve similar tasks. A red light always means "stop." A green light always means "go."

Accommodating how guests think, respond, and contribute to an immersive experience is a critical part of your storyplexing toolbox. You cannot build a successful experience if you disregard the participants.

ACTUALLY, IT'S WHERE YOU SHOULD BEGIN.

CREATING A STORYPLEX

What steps should you take when you're ready to begin creating an immersive experience?

A storyteller might be tempted to pull out a piece of paper and start jotting down characters or plot events. Engineers might be compelled to launch Unity and begin placing objects in a 3D environment. Artists might prepare sketches of the look and feel of the world they wish to create.

Resist the urge to fall back on the familiar. Over years of creating immersive projects, I have found the following approach helps to anchor me and my teams in immersive thinking.

Start with Psychology

If you start building your immersive experience around a story, the temptation will be to tell the audience something. Storyplexes begin with the guests' presence in the space and a sensation being conveyed. Until it is second nature to do so, take the time, every time, to transition into the storyplexing mindset, shifting from Square to Spherical mentality. Establish a vocabulary that encourages immersive thinking. We

> "EVERYTHING YOU SEE OR HEAR OR EXPERIENCE IN ANY WAY AT ALL IS SPECIFIC TO YOU. YOU CREATE A UNIVERSE BY PERCEIVING IT, SO EVERYTHING IN THE UNIVERSE YOU PERCEIVE IS SPECIFIC TO YOU."
> —DOUGLAS ADAMS

live in and interact with a world filled with frames. It is natural to cling to a square mentality. Relinquish control and replace it with the psychology of the participant.

To help place yourselves in their mindset, begin with something you are already intimately familiar with, have daily access to, and can tap into anytime: yourself. Look at your experience not as though you were telling a story, but as if you were inside the experience already. Mentally transport yourself into an imaginary landscape and consider how you can elicit story elements: plot, character, thought, diction, song, spectacle. Start with what you want the world to feel like, what is important to convey, and what it means to be in that environment.

Even the simplest interactions are often overlooked by immersive creators clinging to the storytelling mindset. If you and I are friendly colleagues, and we happen to randomly see each other on Fifth Avenue in New York, we would make eye contact and perhaps stop and chat a bit. That simple interaction of acknowledgment, of establishing a guest's existence, is frequently neglected by creators. When creators ignore a guest's presence in a virtual environment and proceed to tell a story as if their audience was looking through a frame, the guest ends up in narrative limbo. Their experience in the virtual world doesn't match conditioned social expectations. They're sensing that they are in an environment, and yet the world and the characters in it carry on as if they didn't exist. Matt Burdette, of the Oculus Story Studio team, called this the "Swayze effect" after the "experiences and struggles of Sam Wheat, the protagonist in *Ghost*, the 1990 hit film starring Patrick Swayze and Demi Moore. Basically, it's the feeling of yelling 'I'm here! I'm here!' when no one or nothing else around seems to acknowledge it." This is not to say that guests must always play a character or role in an experience, but that considering the psychological state that the guest enters the experience with puts creatives in the mindset of building a world rather than telling a story.

Going back to the psychology of an immersive experience can also help guide your decisions during production. In 2015, U.S. President Barack Obama visited Nairobi, Kenya, for the first time during his presidency. He was to give a speech about African entrepreneurship, the treatment of women, and his high expectations for the Africa of the future. I was invited to film this historic speech in 360. Because the space would not be navigable in the final experience, the choice of where to put the camera inside the Coliseum where the president would be speaking was the most important decision I had to make. Its position relative to certain key elements would determine the context of the story. For security reasons, being upfront and close to the president wasn't an option. That was an angle traditionally covered by news outlets who could use various camera angles and zoom lenses to craft a highly polished editorialized newsreel that 360 content couldn't compete with. So I went back to thinking about what kind of psychological experience I wanted to convey.

As soon as we had walked into the Coliseum, the dynamic energy of citizens and authorities alike was electrifying. Kenyans danced and sang as they waited, constantly checking their cellphones and taking pictures. They never sat down. Meanwhile press outlets stacked into stands that reminded me of a high school gymnasium. BBC and local Kenyan broadcast stations stood alongside podcasters and radio announcers. They knew the world's eyes were on Kenya.

Placing the camera on the press risers would give us a direct eye-line to President Obama, a view of the prominent Kenyan figures below us on the floor, and proximity to the press interpretations of the speech, while also capturing everyday citizens in the balcony behind us.

This experience would transport guests into the world of the Kenyans on this historic day. Guests could choose to watch a Kenyan citizen's body language, see how the security kept track of the crowds, and be dramatically close to reporters usually hidden behind cameras, all while listening to the President's speech.

This choice paid off the moment President Obama took the stage. Simultaneously, as the leader of the free world entered, the Kenyans in the balcony roared and cheered, the dignitaries stood to clap respectfully, and the BBC reporter who had covered events all over the world couldn't help but smile at the contagious energy.

The position of the 360 camera created a perspective that allowed multiple narratives to take place concurrently. The viewer would ultimately decide which perspective was most interesting and relevant to them, and construct the narrative that they wanted out of the experience.

The psychology of going beyond the frame can be externally driven by what the guest choses to interact with or it can be explored by creatives within the experience itself. I tried this with another 360 video project I developed with InceptionVR called *Monet in Giverny: The Later Years*.

When we first started discussing a Monet 360 experience, I researched existing immersive projects on visual artists and realized that they all mirrored the framed mindset. Museum walls were faithfully reconstructed inside virtual worlds to replicate institutions such as the Louvre and the British Museum. In the headset, guests would stand in the virtual building to view a virtual painting on a wall, just as they might in real life. Other visual art experiences, such as *The Night Cafe* and *Dreams of Dali*, allowed guests to go "into" a painting on the wall.

With *Monet in Giverny: The Later Years*, a 360 animation–live action hybrid, I wanted to explore Claude Monet's paintings in a way that couldn't be done in framed mediums: to see the world through the artist's eyes. To do this we first recorded a live-action stereoscopic 3D capture of Monet's garden in Giverny, France, at the exact vantage point from which he painted his iconic "The Artist's House from the Rose Garden." This painting was created towards the end of Monet's life, when his eyesight was failing. Cataracts altered the colors he saw in the world and, consequently, the palette of his paintings. In the immersive experience, the landscape gradually shifted from the garden's natural blues and greens to red-yellows, reflecting the artist's own affliction of a limited visual palette. Then streaks of color animated in, designed to replicate the master's painting techniques. Veteran Broadway actor Merwin Foard voiced Monet's thoughts, which had been painstakingly reconstructed from archived letters and interviews. Stroke after stroke, the painting coalesces into the familiar masterpiece, but now the audience saw its completion through the eyes of an aging and frustrated artist. *Monet in Giverny: The Later Years* explored art as an intimate psychological process rather than a final product.

Expanding beyond frames and museum walls breathes new life into familiar masterpieces and invigorates our sense of connection to them. We can inspire audiences and artists with the magical confluence of art, vision, and circumstance. Just as Monet expressed an object not by painting it exactly as it appeared, but by capturing impressions of its essence, virtual reality is capable of much more than realistic replication.

We all have the innate ability to storyplex by tapping our own experiences. We place ourselves in the guests' shoes and ask

STORYPLEXING EXERCISE

Without thinking about the technology or the story, try describing the experience that you want to build in terms of inclinations and sensations. Without a pencil in hand or a laptop open, and before any story is being told, mentally and emotionally outline the experience or spheres of experiences.

ourselves *why* we do things, *what* constraints we have, and *how* we overcome them.

Determine your Scope

Not long ago, I was approached by executives at a medical device company who wanted to optimize the implementation of their products in hospitals and reduce the number of errors that occurred when installing their devices. Attracted to the attention VR had been getting in the medical community, they decided they wanted to create a VR handbook that would be distributed with Google Cardboards when their product shipped. I invited them to describe what they envisioned happening when someone experienced their VR application, *i.e.* Start with Psychology. As they explained situations that required nurses to be able to see the real world, use their hands, and evaluate their performance, it was clear that if immersive technology was to be used, an AR solution was more appropriate than VR. We shifted over and reviewed AR technologies. The ones that suited their needs were more difficult to distribute and cost more than the client was ready to spend. So what did I suggest? Go back to distributing a printed checklist or create a simple follow-along app that the nurses could refer to. What they wanted to do with immersive technology either didn't suit their needs or was out of their budget. Imagine the headache they saved by not jumping right in and hiring a VR team.

You'll notice that two things influenced my client's technology selection: distribution and budget. If you began your immersive journey thinking "I want to make a 360 video!" but find that the experience you're envisioning requires interactivity, you may find yourself changing your choice of technology to suit the needs of the project.

Determining how you will distribute the experience to an audience will have a significant impact on the technology you use. If you want broad distribution to as many people as possible, then the optimal technology will be different than if you want to show it at a handful of conferences. *The Game of Thrones: Ascend the Wall* VR experience was only available during the 2014 SXSW conference. By limiting the distribution, the creators were able to focus on creating a complex installation optimized for a thrilling experience. Guests who entered the experience were put into an elevator resembling the HBO television series. Inside VR headsets, they rode to the top of the dramatic heights of the iconic Wall and could walk along, looking out at the vast North. During the experience, wind machine and rumble packs activated, creating a sensational installation that was hailed in the press and across social media. On the other hand, Owlchemy Lab's *Job Simulator,* a humorous VR experience where humans can learn how to "job," was released on the popular online game platform Steam across all HMD platforms. The relatively unknown studio earned over 3 million dollars, one of the top-selling VR experiences in 2017. Augmented reality applications face a similar distribution bottleneck. If distributed through smartphones, they have the potential to reach millions of customers. The AR game *Pokemon Go* game has been downloaded 752 million times so far. However, these experiences are confined to the constraints of a smartphone. AR headsets offer a more compelling and useful hands-free solution, but lack wide distribution. Microsoft said that their 2016 sales of the Hololens AR HMD only reached the thousands.

Development options will often be dictated by budget. You may want to build a photo-realistic, interactive experience and find that you only have the budget for a 360 video, which has happened with many of my clients. You might want to release that video on every conceivable mobile platform, but your budget might dictate that the experience be released only on iOS, Apple's proprietary operating system for the market-dominating iPhone.

With these determinations in place, identify your timeframe. If this is a passion project with no deadline, you can indulge in learning and developing as you go. A tight deadline will reduce

STORYPLEXING EXERCISE

Once you've consulted a VR specialist to determine which technology to use, spend several hours experiencing what others have built with it. Download comparable projects onto your smartphone, visit a VR arcade, or block "experience time" out at your office on the Hololens. Take mental notes of what works and what doesn't. This will help you make decisions during your own development.

your development time or require you to expand your team. Your scope includes distribution, budget, timeframe, and technology.

Diversify your Thinking

Whether you are a solo classical artist with no experience in game engines or a business executive with the resources to put together an extensive team, one factor will be the key force for creating a powerful experience: diversity. Be diverse in your team, in your skillset, and in your thinking.

If you are working independently, tap into existing communities who are creating immersive environments and explore them with vigor. Download and watch as many experiences as you can, on as many devices as you have access to. Step beyond 360 videos and go to a VR arcade and spend hours trying different types of content. Attend a local meet-up group and surround yourself with people from different backgrounds and skill sets.

If you are assembling a team for the project, diversify the skillsets and perspectives you are onboarding. Make sure the team isn't a film crew or an engineering squad. Know your strengths and surround yourself with people from different knowledge banks. The ability to assemble a large team is an opportunity to expand your powerbase further to include all genders, cultures, and ages. This isn't to meet diversity quotas or appear politically correct. A diverse team will dramatically enhance your ability to design and build a powerful experience for a wider audience. Our experiences, beliefs, knowledge, and circumstances give each one of us a unique perspective for problem-solving.

A foundational mantra in Human–Computer Interaction design is: *Know thy User, for they are Not You.* This principle reflects the diversity of human nature and embraces how diversity can improve our designs. We all have a tendency to make assumptions about how a guest will behave in an environment based on our own experiences, but cultural differences, experience level, and physical conditions all impact how a system is used. Creating immersive experiences has the double whammy of needing to construct a product with assumptions on both the interface and narrative. Take away the frame and incorporate interactivity, and suddenly accommodating human behavior becomes vitally important. Usability experts will design a system to support a wide variety of human behaviors, and so should creators. As immersive thinkers, we must be inclusive thinkers. We must actively pursue perspectives from different genders, ethnicities, backgrounds, ages, and philosophies.

STORYPLEXING EXERCISE

Great minds don't have to think alike, but on a development project they do need to be able to think together. Who do you know, or want to know, that would compliment and expand your skillset and knowledge base? Don't be afraid to reach out. Most immersive creators I know are deeply fascinated by the medium and excited to share their knowledge with people entering the space.

Create a Spatial Map

Okay, you've gathered your interdisciplinary team or resources, and are focused on the psychology of the experience, with a clear vision of the scope you'll be working in. Now can you retrieve a pen from the drawer or power-up the word processing software? Not yet! Before confining ourselves to the almighty page, if this is unfamiliar territory for you, I highly suggest you design the experience and its interactions in a way that allows you to make mistakes quickly and think through solutions spatially.

Mapping a design is similar to novelists jotting down plot ideas on index cards to structure and restructure the outlines without feeling obligated to one idea or another. Author Blake Snyder, in his popular book on screenwriting, *Save the Cat*, articulates a narrative structure that strictly follows page numbers. The set-up for the movie is contained in pages 1-10. The catalyst moment occurs on page 12. From pages 12-25, the thematic dilemma is debated. And so forth. In an interactive system, instead of a single linear plot, HCI flow charts and task analysis outlines take into account when and how the user interacts with content. For intricate and involved systems, these are critical. For less complex or narrative-based experiences, a simplified version of these can be very helpful in moving thoughts away from the page and into physical space.

Sketching out ideas lets you develop and iterate without the time and expense of development. A spatial map is a way of prototyping without technology, a visual guide to the interfaces and interactions that create an experience.

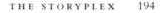

In 2018, educators from MIT, UPenn, Johns Hopkins, Florida International University, Stanford, Case Western, Yale, and a dozen more universities actively incorporating virtual reality into their curriculums, met at a summit in New Haven where I had only an hour to workshop thinking immersively with them. The most transformative step in the process is often the transition from sequential thinking to spatial thinking. I asked attendees to break out into groups and gave them sticky notes to use to design an immersive experience. Most participants placed the sticky notes as a linear sequence of events or actions prescribed for the guest. This happens every time I lead this exercise. But by working in a three-dimensional space rather than writing a concept on paper, the tendency to outline a linear story becomes immediately apparent. By using sticky notes, they can rearrange the notes as they transition into thinking spatially.

Spatial mapping allows a team to think through the guest experience and integrate a narrative into the environment that is responsive in the Aristotelean *propter hoc* sense, where events occur "because of" each other or the guest's interactions. Design needs, interaction constraints, spatial layouts, navigation modes and more can be tackled through sticky notes before committing to a specific build.

This lengthy, iterative process results in a design document that provides an overview of what the system needs to do. From here, implementation can begin.

Build

When you are ready to implement your spatial map, a multitude of resources on creating immersive content are available online—from filming in 360, working in Unity, designing interactivity and user experience. Your greatest impact, however, will come from the interdisciplinary team executing the vision.

Generally speaking, production pipelines today largely depend on the visual display system to which the experience will be delivered. Virtual environments intended for linear displays (360 video, mobile VR) typically look like film pipelines. Spherical content is brought into non-linear editing software such as Adobe Premiere where it is "unwrapped" into an equirectangular format that allows the editor to view the entire landscape inside a single reference frame. Footage is cut, adjusted, and color-corrected similar to filmmaking. Audio is layered in, and the final version is exported for viewing. The downfall in following a film-based post-production is a tendency to fall back on telling a story. If the display will be interactive (mobile VR, HMD), projects tend to follow a game-development process. These pipelines lean heavily on building the world in a game engine through designing and placing assets, and coding and debugging scripts. Ambitious or well-funded projects may use a hybrid of these.

Along the way, there may be trade-offs and moments where the initial vision is compromised because of technological constraints, budget, or deadlines. Or perhaps you need to take time to innovate the technology to adapt it to your needs. The most important thing to remember in the build stage is that each section of the toolbox—the technology, the creatives, and the participants—should balance as the experience evolves. *The technology shouldn't drive the experience to the exclusion of storylines or participants.* If you discover that the narrative you've designed doesn't work when people enter your experience, then adjust the design to reduce errors. Which brings me to the next very important step in storyplexing, one which should always be integrated into the build process.

Test, Analyze, and Iterate. Repeat.

Both classical and immersive creators test their creations, but in very different ways. In a traditional storytelling process, the writer or director iterates with themselves or their team. Film directors sit in dark editing rooms with their engineers. Theatre companies rehearse on closed stages. Writers send pages back and forth to their editor. The audience is rarely included in these sessions.

By contrast, immersive creators should put their creations in the hands of guests early and often. When guests interact with immersive content, even the most basic functionality of looking around an environment can change the experience from one person to the next. Inevitably, guests act differently than we expect them to. Experienced immersive designers know guests will come to the experience with a wide variety of expectations, experiences and desires. They plan for it. They test for it by having people try the system. And then they go back into development. Confusing interactions are re-designed. Sometimes entirely new interfaces are needed. When new implementations of the experience are ready, the revised version goes back out for a new round of testing. Iterative design is crucial for moving out of the auteur mindset and making allowances for agency.

As a mentor in the Facebook/Oculus VR for Good program through Digital Promise, I mentored high-school teachers and students creating 360 video experiences, many of them for the first time. Each semester dozens of 360 projects are conceptualized, filmed, edited and submitted. When they are submitted, I can easily tell which group of students never looked at their footage in a headset or tested the footage with someone besides themselves. Typical tell-tale signs are title cards that look fine on frame in an editing suite but are unreadable in a headset, extreme camera movement that looks cool in film but is nauseating when immersed in it, and jump cuts seen in classic music videos that are impossible to follow in VR. In each case, if the students had watched the footage from within a headset at any given point in the process, they would have immediately recognized they had a problem.

Testing doesn't need to be elaborate and expansive. A study done by HCI guru Jakob Nielsen of the Nielsen Norman Group found that the majority of interface problems will be identified by your first five users:

As soon as you collect data from a single test user, your insights shoot up and you have already learned almost a third of all there is to know about the usability of the design. The difference between zero and even a little bit of data is astounding.

When you test the second user, you will discover that this person does some of the same things as the first user, so there is some overlap in what you learn. People are definitely different, so there will also be something new that the second user does that you did not observe with the first user. So the second user adds some amount of new insight, but not nearly as much as the first user did.

The third user will do many things that you already observed with the first user or with the second user and even some things that you have already seen twice. Plus, of course, the third user will generate a small amount of new data, even if not as much as the first and the second user did.

As you add more and more users, you learn less and less because you will keep seeing the same things again and again. There is no real need to keep observing the same thing multiple times, and you will be very motivated to go back to the drawing board and redesign the site to eliminate the usability problems.

After the fifth user, you are wasting your time by observing the same findings repeatedly but not learning much new.

Dr. Nielsen suggests that rather than conducting one test with 15 subjects, a design will benefit more from doing three tests with five subjects each. After each test, iterate the design, make a

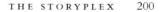

change, and then put that new design back in front of more guests.

I find that when speakers or developers declare that "no one knows what the answer is" after working with immersive technology, they often took the auteur approach with a Square mindset and implemented a singular vision without testing and iterating.

STORYPLEXING EXERCISE

Testing can be as simple as asking a colleague to try the experience in whatever state it is in. Don't give them instructions on how to interact or make excuses about the state of the demonstration. Just place someone who is unfamiliar with the project in the experience and silently observe their actions as they go through it. Watch what they do, when they have difficulties, as well as how they solve those problems. Afterwards, ask them open-ended questions about what made sense, what didn't, where they got lost, and what they enjoyed.

Learn and Share

When VR was largely an academic pursuit, researchers from all mediums were exploring its potential, writing papers, and sharing discoveries. Organizations such as SIGCHI, SIGGRAPH, and IEEE were built for the purpose of expanding and distributing knowledge. Now corporations file wide-reaching patents daily, colleagues are sworn to secrecy by iron-clad NDAs, and the spirit of learning and sharing begins to be choked by the need to capitalize and the desire to stake a claim in the history books of VR, AR, and MR. I suppose this trade-off is somewhat inevitable, and I really do find immense enjoyment in seeing new generations of developers and students have access to immersive technology and helping each other learn.

As we explore and expand, remember that innovation thrives on sharing our discoveries and explorations. Whether approaching immersive experiences as a content creator, a business executive, or a curious audience member, our journey begins where our assumptions about story*telling* ends.

THE STORYPLEXING CREATOR

As the excitement mounted and the money poured into the virtual and augmented reality industries after Facebook bought Oculus in 2014, the media hotly debated the promise of virtual reality. Impulse articles and endless buzzwords asked: Is VR the "next big thing?" Followed by "is AR the 'next big thing?'" Is it all hype? When will it all come crashing down?

While most of the attention centered around the technology itself, industry leaders, including Oculus CTO John Carmack, recognized that powerful hardware isn't enough to build a sustainable industry. For immersive technology to succeed, the devices must have compelling content. Even with new VR and AR companies launching almost daily, investments flowing in, and major studios setting up shop, the industry consensus was that the content created for this revolutionary technology had stagnated. When the 2016 forecasts of adoption rate for VR fell below analysts' expectations, fingers were pointed at the high cost of equipment and the lack of compelling content. Hardware manufacturers have steadily dropped the prices of hardware components, but the experiences have remained largely lackluster. Games were ported to the headsets without being redesigned for the medium. Branded experiences clung to old business formulas for success, hoping to repeat it without investing in research. Without content that people *want* to engage with, without experiences that stimulate them in meaningful and powerful ways, it doesn't matter what the technology is capable of or has potential to become.

We must think immersively, build worlds, and guide our guests towards the future. The dilemma we now find ourselves in is that the potential of the technology is limited by our imaginations, which are in turn largely limited by our established paradigms.

The systems and structures currently in place support a world that preceded immersive technology. Creators on this path will insist on applying knowledge of previous mediums as de facto solutions in exchange for a temporary spotlight.

Immersive technology approached as an exploration of ideas reconnects us with our conscious center and seeks a higher truth that brings us closer to ourselves and our humanity. This is the path to Ivan Sutherland's Wonderland: uniting human experience with computer programming. Moving beyond premeditated stories that authors contrive for audiences to witness, it seeks Plato's Form: the essence of humanity that is more true than its representation in books, films, paintings, or worldly objects. It asks, "were you not constrained by the physics of the real world, what would you experience?" The challenge is not to justify the technology in today's context, but to envision the potential of what lies beyond our current constraints.

When we shift into creating immersive worlds, immersive creators are not the author who writes word after word of prose. They are not the painter who brushes stroke after stroke onto a canvas. They are not film directors who plot the audio-visual layout of a script onto a 16x9 frame. Those are tools and techniques of classical storytellers, which will evolve. History has shown that our audiences will also evolve. They will not be the audiences who sat back passively, staring into frames or experiencing content from a distance. They will join us on this journey.

Those who can make the cognitive shift into immersive thinking, and transcend pre-existing assumptions about how the world is supposed to work, will lead the charge in in changing the world—and the craft of narrative—as we know it.

■ ■　　■ ■ ■　　■ ■ ■ ■　　■ ■ ■ ■　　■ ■ ■ ■

AS YOU FORGE INTO UNFAMILIAR TERRITORY, THE URGE WILL LIKELY BE TO FALL BACK INTO COMFORTABLE TECHNIQUES OF *classical* MEDIUMS:

TO DRAFT THE *script*, TO TELL A **story**.

If you feel this fear,
DIG DEEPER.

BACK TO WHEN YOU WERE A CHILD.
WHEN ANYTHING WAS POSSIBLE.

CONSIDER THIS THE EDGE OF YOUR
IMAGINARY FORTRESS.

THE EVOLUTION OF IMMERSIVE NARRATIVES WILL BE AS MUCH ADVANCEMENTS OF

TECHNOLOGY

AS THEY ARE

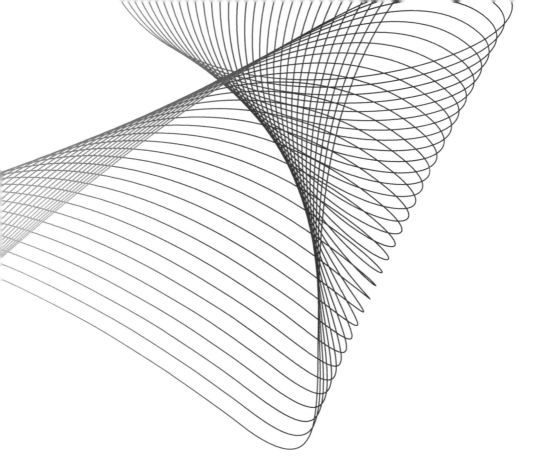

FEATS OF THE
IMAGINATION.

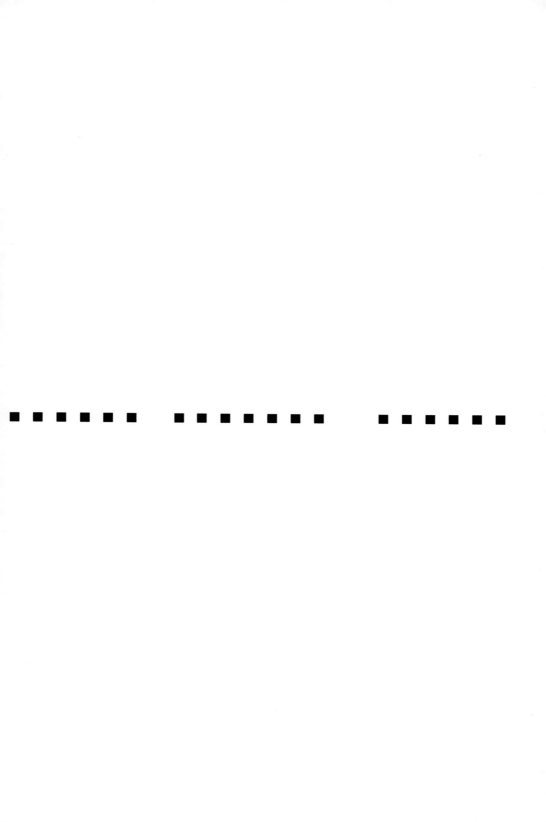

ENDNOTES

PROLOGUE

The fascinating story of Chester Carlton's invention and the circumstances around its denial and development is thoroughly detailed in *David Owen's book, Copies in Seconds: How a Lone Inventor and an Unknown Company Created the Biggest Communication Breakthrough Since Gutenberg—Chester Carlson and the Birth of the Xerox Machine* (Simon & Schuster, 2004).

Lord Kelvin is quoted as saying both "Heavier-than-air flying machines are impossible" (1895) and "I have not the smallest molecule of faith in aerial navigation other than ballooning" (1896) in Anton Z. Capri's book *Quips, Quotes, and Quanta: An Anecdotal History of Physics*, 2nd Edition (World Scientific Publishing Company, May 31, 2011, Chapter 4: It's about Time and Space).

Charles Darwin explains his expectations of rebuttal directly in his seminal work *On The Origin of Species by Means of Natural Selection, or Preservation of Favoured Races in the Struggle for Life* (London:John Murray, 1859).

Helge Kragh in his 2000 article for *Physics World*, "Max Planck: the reluctant revolutionary," explored how "Planck's role in the discovery of quantum theory was complex and somewhat ambiguous."

"Lumière's *Arrival of the Train*, Cinema's Founding Myth," written by Martin Loiperdinger for *The Moving Image* journal challenged many assumptions about the reportings of the Lumière films. The Moving Image 4(1), 89-118. University of Minnesota Press from Project MUSE database.

IMMERSIVE TECHNOLOGY CHEATSHEET

The diagram and context for Paul Milgram's reality-virtuality continuum can be found in his original paper, "Augmented Reality: A class of displays on the reality-virtuality continuum", written with H. Takemura, A. Utsumi, and F. Kishino and published in *Proceedings of Telemanipulator and Telepresence Technologies* (1994).

Guinness World Records Gamer's Edition 2008 holds the Wii Sports record for "Hardware: Best-Sellers by Platform". Craig Glenday, ed. *Guinness World Records*. (Guinness, 2008).

THE STORYTELLING PROBLEM

A thorough history of Thespis' role in Greek Theatre is contained in *Theatre of the Greeks* by Philip Wentworth Buckham. (Cambridge: J. Smith, 1827).

Charles Francis Jenkins first published an article on "Motion Pictures by Wireless—Wonderful possibilities of Motion Picture

Progress" in *Moving Picture News* on September 27, 1913.
Twelve years later, on June 30, 1925, he was granted a patent for
"Transmitting Pictures over Wireless".

I highly recommend reading the entirety of Janet H. Murray's
book *Hamlet on the Holodeck: The Future of Narrative in Cyberspace*
as a provocative and thorough exploration of the intersection
of technology and narrative through an academic perspective
(Cambridge, MA: MIT Press, 1997).

Morton Heilig's complete essay, "The Cinema of the Future"
(1955) can be found in *Multimedia: From Wagner to Virtual Reality*
by Randall Packer, Ken Jordan, William Gibson, and Laurie
Anderson. (New York: W. W. Norton & Company, 2006).

Powerful examples of presence span decades, independent of
the hardware or software available. The ones referenced here are
excerpted from the paper "The Experience of Presence: Factor
Analytic Insights" by Thomas Schubert, Frank Friedmann, and
Holger Regenbrecht in the journal *Presence: Teleoperators and
Virtual Environments 10*, no. 3 (2001): 266-81; John Patrick
Pullen's January 8, 2016 *Time.com* article, "I Finally Tried Virtual
Reality and It Brought Me to Tears"; Daniel Goleman's June 21,
1995 article "'Virtual Reality' Conquers Fear of Heights" in *The
New York Times*; the 2008 paper "Observing Virtual Arms That You
Imagine Are Yours Increases the Galvanic Skin Response to an
Unexpected Threat" by Karin Hägni, Kynan Eng, Marie-Claude

Hepp-Reymond, Lisa Holper, Birgit Keisker, Ewa Siekierka, and Daniel C. Kiper. *PLoS ONE* 3, no. 8; and Carrie Heeter's paper "Being There: The subjective experience of presence," *Presence: Teleoperators and Virtual Environments*. (MIT Press, fall, 1992).

Brian Ferren's quote, "If you're trying to tell a story, you don't want the audience deciding where it should go, that's why you have a director and producer," is one of many gems and fascinating observations about how narrative is evolving through technology in scholar Frank Rose's book *The Art of Immersion: How the Digital Generation Is Remaking Hollywood, Madison Avenue, and the Way We Tell Stories*. (New York: W. W. Norton, 2012).

"From Linear Story Generation to Branching Story Graphs," the research paper by Mark Riedel and R. Michael Young, articulates the limitations of a scripted story and the promise of generative narratives. *IEEE Computer Graphics and Applications* 26, no. 3 (2006): 23-31. doi:10.1109/mcg.2006.56.

The Evolution of Verse premiered at Sundance Film Festival in 2015 and can be viewed at https://www.with.in/watch/C7BNx9Q.

Help! won the 2016 Cannes Lions Gold Lion award for Virtual Reality and Technological Achievement. It has over 3.5 million views on YouTube. See: https://www.youtube.com/watch?v=G-XZhKqQAHU

Look in Tom Sito's book *Moving Innovation: A History of Computer Animation* provides anecdotal accounts of the culture of Xerox PARC in the chapter on "Xerox PARC and Corporate Culture" for more insights into this unique culture (Cambridge, MA: MIT Press, 2015).

Viewpoints Research Institute published Dr. Alan Kay's February 24, 2004 remarks on "The Power of the Context", which he presented upon being awarded the Charles Stark Draper Prize of the National Academy of Engineering, along with Bob Taylor, Butler Lampson and Chuck Thacker. A copy can be found online at http://www.vpri.org/pdf/m2004001_power.pdf.

Dr. Alan Kay wrote a wonderful response to a question on Quora "What Made Xerox PARC Special? Who Else Today Is like Them?" on April 5, 2017. https://www.quora.com/What-made-Xerox-PARC-special-Who-else-today-is-like-them/answer/Alan-Kay-11.

The visionary paper, "A Personal Computer for Children of All Ages," by Dr. Alan Kay was first published on August 1, 1972 in the ACM '72 Proceedings of the *ACM Annual Conference* 1, no. 1. In the aforementioned "The Power of the Context" remarks, Dr. Kay cites Ivan Sutherland's paper, "Sketchpad a Man-Machine Graphical Communication System." Simulation 2, no. 5 (1964). Ivan Sutherland's inspiration of Vannevar Bush's 1945 article in *The Atlantic*, "As We May Think" is mentioned at https://en.wikipedia.org/wiki/Ivan_Sutherland.

I've heard the quote "the best way to predict the future is to invent it" several different ways. Here I cite Dr. Alan Kay as quoted by the periodical *InfoWorld* on August 16, 1982, Volume 4, Number 16, "Experts speculate on future electronic learning environment" by Deborah Wise, Page 6, Published by InfoWorld Media Group, Inc.

WHAT'S OLD IS NEW AGAIN

Examples of societies' bizarre responses to technology can be found in Ben Rooney's article "Women And Children First: Technology And Moral Panic" *Wall Street Journal*, July 11, 2011. https://blogs.wsj.com/tech-europe/2011/07/11/women-and-children-first-technology-and-moral-panic/.

The multinational networking and telecommunications company Ericsson chronicles the history of the telephone on their website, including early responses to it in the article, "The telephone is the instrument of the devil". See: https://www.ericsson.com/en/about-us/history/communication/how-the-telephone-changed-the-world/the-telephone-is-the-instrument-of-the-devil

Anton A. Huudeman's book *The Worldwide History of Telecommunications* documents the folly of the Western Union committee assigned to review Bell's offer of the rights to the telephone for $100,000 by reporting that the voice was very "weak and indistinct" and "hardly more than a toy" before recommending not to purchase the rights. (Wiley IEEE Press Imprint, 2003, p165).

The president of Michigan Savings Bank in 1903 is widely quoted as telling Henry Ford's lawyer, Horace Rackham, not to invest in the automobile company by saying, "The horse is here to stay, but the automobile is only a novelty—a fad." https://en.wikipedia.org/wiki/Horace_Rackham

Eadward Muybridge's experiments have been well documented in scientific journals, articles and books, including Stephen Herbert's book *The Man Who Stopped Time: The Illuminating Story of Eadweard Muybridge—Pioneer Photographer, Father of the Motion Picture, Murderer.* (Early Popular Visual Culture 7, no. 1. 2009).

Watch Ivan Sutherland talk about the experiments at Bell Helicopter when he realized he could substitute a computer for a camera at the 2015 Proto Awards here: https://www.theverge.com/2015/10/8/9479129/ivan-sutherland-proto-awards-virtual-reality-speech.

Ivan Sutherland's complete essay, "The Ultimate Display" (1965) can be found in *Multimedia: From Wagner to Virtual Reality* by Randall Packer, Ken Jordan, William Gibson, and Laurie Anderson (New York: W.W. Norton & Company, 2006).

Berenice Abbott wrote "Photography can never grow up if it imitates some other medium. It has to walk alone; it has to be itself" in 1951, captured in the Dec 11, 1991 *The New York Times* retrospective article "Berenice Abbott, 93, Dies; Her Photographs Captured New York in Transition."

Oksana Bulgakowa and David Bordwell explored Vertov's editing in their article "The Ear against the Eye: Vertov's 'Symphony'" published in *Monatshefte*, Vol. 98, No. 2, The Art of Hearing (Summer, 2006, pp. 219-243).

Aristotle's "Poetics" can be explored in full online at MIT's Internet Classics Archive, translated by S. H. Butcher http://classics.mit.edu/Aristotle/poetics.html

Film Technique and Film Acting by Vsevolod I. Pudovkin and Ivor Goldsmid Samuel is available in reprint (New York: Bonanza Books, 2007).

The decline of the piano is beautifully explored in Paul Kendall's 2013 article for *The Telegraph* and can be read online at https://www.telegraph.co.uk/culture/music/music-news/9813479/How-we-fell-out-of-tune-with-the-piano.html

Marshall McLuhan's quote comes from his pivotal work, *The Medium Is the Massage: An Inventory of Effects*, which he constructed with Quentin Fiore, and Jerome Agel. (New York, Bantan Books, 1967).

Historical data on the flags flown over the Globe Theatre can be found at http://www.bardstage.org/globe-theatre-flags.htm

Christopher Vogler expanded his original essay into a full book with Michele Montez entitled *The Writer's Journey: Mythic Structure for Writers*, and republished it with Michael Wiese Productions, 2007. Joseph Campbell's influential *The Hero with a Thousand Faces* was first issued in 1949 and is now available as *The Hero with a Thousand Faces (The Collected Works of Joseph Campbell)* (Novato, CA: New World Library, 2008).

George Lucas discusses the importance of story over visual effects in the 1983 PBS television documentary *From Star Wars to Jedi: The Making of a Saga*.

Dr. Paul J. Zak's scientific approach to understanding storytelling through neuroscience spans multiple articles and books, including "Why inspiring stories make us react: the neuroscience of narrative" (Cerebrum : the Dana forum on brain science vol. 2015 2. 2 Feb. 2015).

According to NASA, "It turns out that roughly 68% of the universe is dark energy. Dark matter makes up about 27%. The rest - everything on Earth, everything ever observed with all of our instruments, all normal matter - adds up to less than 5% of the universe." https://science.nasa.gov/astrophysics/focus-areas/what-is-dark-energy

King, Stephen. *On Writing: A Memoir of the Craft*. London: Hodder & Stoughton, 2000.

Several examples of interactions with Joseph Weizenbaum's computer program ELIZA are contained in his paper "ELIZA—a Computer Program for the Study of Natural Language Communication between Man and Machine." (*Communications of the ACM 9*, no. 1. 1966: 36-45).

THE STORYPLEX

Ed Catmull's insight was made to *The Guardian* in 2015 following Oculus founder Palmer Luckey making "the case for the potential of for virtual reality storytelling" at the Web Summit conference. The article entitled "Pixar co-founder warns virtual-reality moviemakers: 'It's not storytelling'" can be found at: https://www.theguardian.com/technology/2015/dec/03/pixar-virtual-reality-storytelling-ed-catmull

The extensive biography of Walt Disney by Neal Gabler, *Walt Disney: Triumph of the American Imagination*, is an insightful and inspiring read. (New York, NY: Random House, 2006).

Harvard Business Review published B. Joseph Pine II and James H. Gilmore's article "Welcome to the Experience Economy" in 1998.

The Makoko Floating School collapsed in 2016. More information on the architect, the project and the demise of the structure, as well as plans for regeneration can be found at http://www.nleworks.com/case/makoko-floating-school/.

While *Pokémon Go* received mixed critical reviews, it was downloaded more than 10 million times within a week of release according to *Sensor Tower* with *The New York Times* declaring "Pokémon Go Brings Augmented Reality to a Mass Audience" on July 11, 2016.

Dean Takahasi's *Venture Beat* article "How Pixar made *Monsters University,* its latest technological marvel" details the technological demands, creative computing and 2,000 machines Pixar uses to create their animations. "All told, it has taken more than 100 million CPU hours to render the film in its final form." (Venture Beat, April 24, 2013).

More information on the documentary film *Angst*, IndieFlix and *Angst: The Panic Attack* VR experience can be found at https://angstmovie.com/.

Holojam in Wonderland was presented at SIGGRAPH 2018, with paper contributions from David Gochfeld, Ken Perlin, Corinne Brenner, Kris Layng, Sebastian Herscher, Connor Defanti, Marta Olko, David Shinn, Stephanie Riggs, and Clara Fernández-Vara. *ACM SIGGRAPH 2018 Art Gallery* on SIGGRAPH 18, 2018.

While my primary source for Walt Disney's historical data is the aforementioned *Walt Disney: Triumph of the American Imagination* by Neal Gabler, a personal account was told by his daughter, Diane Disney Miller's article, as told to Pete Martin, for *The Saturday Evening Post* series "My Dad, Walt Disney" on December 22, 1956, which is online: http://www.saturdayeveningpost.com/wp-content/uploads/satevepost/Disneys-Folly1.pdf

Vachon, Christine, and Austin Bunn. *A Killer Life*. New York: Limelight, 2007.

Disney's "Four Keys" can be found throughout staff communications in every Disney theme park. There's a succinct outline of them in the Disneyland Paris careers page. See http://careers.disneylandparis.com/en/safety-courtesy-show-and-efficiency-our-four-keys.

Hench, John, and Peggy Van Pelt. *Designing Disney: Imagineering and the Art of the Show*. New York: Disney Editions, 2009.

Because Donald A. Norman's book *The Design of Everyday Things* focuses primarily on designing interactions with everyday objects, it is highly relevant for designing how we interact with objects in virtual worlds. He outlines more principles than I mention here and although I focused on ones I view to be the most relevant to immersive technology, this entire book and all the principles should be taken into consideration. (London: Basic Books, 1988).

The 360 footage of President Barack Obama's speech in Nairobi were part of an experience called *Kanju*, produced by The Nantucket Project, which premiered at Tribeca Film Festival in 2016 and is available to view on JauntVR https://www.jauntvr.com/title/70c9cfb927.

Monet in Giverny: The Later Years was released by InceptionVR in 2017. See https://inceptionvr.com/experience/monet/.

The Game of Thrones: Ascend the Wall experience was created by Framestore. More information and photos of the activation are on their website: https://www.framestore.com/work/ascend-wall-vr-experience.

"The Swayze Effect" article by Matt Burdette was published on the Oculus Story Studio blog on November 18, 2015. https://www.oculus.com/story-studio/blog/the-swayze-effect/

Job Simulator developer Owlchemy Labs reported crossing the 3 million dollar mark on January 6, 2017. https://owlchemylabs.com/job-simulator-sales-milestone/

While "Know Thy User, For They Are Not You" is a familiar mantra in usability, Raluca Budiu explores the reasoning behind it in the article "You Are Not the User: The False-Consensus Effect," which was published on the Neilsen Norman Group blog on October 22, 2017. https://www.nngroup.com/articles/false-consensus/

Snyder, Blake. *Save the Cat!: The Last Book on Screenwriting You'll Ever Need*. Studio City, CA: M. Wiese Productions, 2005.

The Neilsen Norman Group maintains an extensive an invaluable library of articles on usability, interaction, and design on their website. "Why You Only Need to Test with 5 Users" was published by Jakob Neilsen on March 19, 2000 (https://www.nngroup.com/articles/why-you-only-need-to-test-with-5-users/) and cites the mathematics behind his claim from the paper: Nielsen, Jakob, and Landauer, Thomas K.: "A mathematical model of the finding of usability problems" *Proceedings of ACM*

INTERCHI'93 Conference (Amsterdam, The Netherlands: 24-29 April 1993), pp. 206-213.

The Hollywood Reporter reported Oculus CTO John Carmack's Connect conference keynote speech in 2015 where he said that virtual reality "content needs the most effort." Followed by a list of partnerships the company was making with "square" content providers—presumably under the assumption that they would best know how to create content in spherical environments. The full article is available online: https://www.hollywoodreporter. com/behind-screen/oculus-cto-says-virtual-reality-827104.

PHOTO CREDITS

"30 Doradus, Tarantula Nebula" NASA, ESA, ESO, D. Lennon and E. Sabbi (ESA/STScI), J. Anderson, S. E. de Mink, R. van der Marel, T. Sohn, and N. Walborn (STScI), N. Bastian (Excellence Cluster, Munich), L. Bedin (INAF, Padua), E. Bressert (ESO), P. Crowther (Sheffield), A. de Koter (Amsterdam), C. Evans (UKATC/STFC, Edinburgh), A. Herrero (IAC, Tenerife), N. Langer (AifA, Bonn), I. Platais (JHU) and H. Sana (Amsterdam).

Commercial Camera Company (1913-06-19), "Commercial Camera Company Photostat advertisement", in Engineering News[1], volume 69, issue 25, New York, New York, USA: Hill Publishing Company, page 6.

Carlson, Chester. US Patent No. 2,297,691, filed 1939.

Glass building photography by Juhasz Imre. Released under Creative Commons CC0.

Heliocentric model from Nicolaus Copernicus' 1543 *De revolutionibus orbium coelestium* (On the Revolutions of the Heavenly Spheres).

Captain Godard's Airship, *Ballon Captif*, 1896 Hungary Millennium Celebrations.

Hands at the *Cuevas de las Manos upon Río Pinturas*, near the town of Perito Moreno in Santa Cruz Province, Argentina. Picture taken by Marianocecowski, 2005.

L. Galvani, 1793. Voltaic pile experiment diagram.

High resolution source images from Pxhere.com, released under Creative Commons CC0. Attributions not available or required.

Sensorama photograph courtesy of Morton and Marianne Heilig Collection, Hugh M. Hefner Moving Image Archive, University of Southern California School of Cinematic Arts.

All other illustrations, Maya P. Lim, 2018.

ACKNOWLEDGMENTS

I am grateful for the colleagues who encouraged me early on to collect my lectures, research, and experience into a form that could be shared with others—Rob Auten, Stina Hamlin, Tommy Honton, Mark Kratter, Carol Silverman and Adaora Udoji. There were several brave souls who weathered early drafts: Sean Akers, Marjorie Censer, Blair Erickson, Susan Fenichell, Tom Gaultney, Ian McCullough, Peter Mandelstam, and Kathryn Muratore—your patience and honesty were indispensable.

The precision and insightfulness of my editor, Megan Hustad, transformed a collection of ideas into a symphony worthy of being shared. The gorgeous graphic representations of the ideas within this book are the brilliance of my book designer, Maya P. Lim, to whom I have a tremendous amount of gratitude for her creative splendor and indefatigable enthusiasm. Many examples came from my consulting practice at Sunchaser Entertainment—Scilla Andreen, Scott A. Jennings, Jeff Phaklides, Em Grosland, Merwin Foard, Dr. Ken Perlin, Dr. Takeo Kanade, Zach Morris, The Nantucket Project and the Disney Imagineers—thank you for letting me share your stories. Denise Quesnel and Jerome Solomon at SIGGRAPH (truly this conference is my happy place), Loren Hammonds at Tribeca Film Festival and Kyle Bergman at the Architecture and Design Film Festival who have always been champions, and Jacques Verly at Stereopsia all spearhead vibrant conferences and gatherings where bold ideas are shared and celebrated, including mine. These were invaluable opportunities to share and evolve ideas with like-minded souls. I am indebted to my colleagues at Yale University, Johannes DeYoung and Justin Berry who graciously supported my philosophical explorations of these emerging mediums.

In the spirit of child-like exploration, I dedicated this book to my mother in her maiden name, Karen Ann Funderburk. Her selfless and loving support throughout my life has been a perpetual source of grounding and strength. My father, Walker Gaultney, emboldened me to push beyond my comfort zone, which I couldn't have written this book without. And my aunt and uncle, Linda and Justin Deedy Jr., have steadied the rollercoaster of life in incalculable ways that made room for this book to be possible. I am forever grateful for the generosity, kindness, creativity, and joy of the exquisite Aléna Watters, the brilliant Tamara Ham, and the courageous Dana Buning—thank you, ladies.

I owe thanks most of all to my partner, Christopher Mecham, and my son, Charlie Gilbert, for our home where love makes space for us to work towards our dreams, where fear cowers in the face of determined passion, and where trust provides the foundation to grow stronger and go farther than we ever thought possible.

ABOUT THE AUTHOR

Photo: Evan Miller

STEPHANIE RIGGS is a former Disney Imagineer whose career spans theatre, film, television, video games, software development, location-based experiences, and immersive technology. Her work has been featured around the world in *The New York Times*, *BBC*, *Al Jazeera*, *Variety*, *The Hollywood Reporter*, and *UploadVR*. She has been invited to speak and present at conferences around the world, including SIGGRAPH, IEEE, World Immersion Forum, Digital Hollywood, Future of Storytelling, and the Tribeca Film Festival. She has collaborated on experiences with GoogleVR, Facebook/Oculus, Netflix, AmazonStudios, InceptionVR, and NYU's Future Realities Lab. Stephanie graduated Phi Beta Kappa from Carnegie Mellon University's School of Drama and School of Computer Science simultaneously and was a consultant at Yale University's Blended Reality Lab at the Center for Collaborative Arts and Media.

Stephanie lives in New York and is the Creative Director of Experiential at Refinery29.